The Broadcast Media Inside Track

The Broadcast Media Inside Track

A Newcomer's Guide to Getting Your Dream Job

BY **BEN ANCHOR**

Illustrations by Natsu Fukano

Copyright © 2021 Ben Anchor
All rights reserved.
ISBN-13: 978-1-8384947-4-2

Table of Contents

ABOUT THE AUTHOR 3
   WHO I AM 3
   HOW I GOT HERE 7
   WHY WRITE A BOOK? 21

INTRODUCTION 25
   IDENTIFYING THE PROBLEM 27
   SEARCH LIKE IT'S A JOB 31
   MAKE A PROMISE 35

THE BROADCAST MEDIA LANDSCAPE 41
   TYPES OF ROLES 41
      CREATIVE 44
      TECHNICAL 44
      OPERATIONAL 45
      COMMERCIAL 45
      PROJECT 46
   TYPES OF COMPANIES 49
      BROADCASTERS 51
      SERVICE PROVIDERS 52
      CONTENT PROVIDERS 53
      PRODUCTION COMPANIES 53

TYPES OF WORK 58
   PAYROLL (PAYE/FTC) V SELF EMPLOYED 60
   STATIC HOURS (OFFICE) V ANTISOCIAL 61
   BROADCAST NICHE V INDUSTRY AGNOSTIC 61
   OTHER PATHS 62

YOUR COMPETENCY - CAN YOU DO THE WORK? 66
   BESPOKE COMPETENCY 68
   PORTFOLIO 72
   YOUR BROADCAST MEDIA CV 75
      CURRICULUM VITAE STYLE 75
   YOUR LINKEDIN MAKEOVER 78
      LINKEDIN STYLE 78

YOUR COMPATIBILITY - CAN YOU DO THE WORK HERE? 82

- INDUSTRY SOURCES 84
- TARGET MATRIX 85
- GROW YOUR NETWORK 86
- GAIN KNOWLEDGE 87
- GET YOURSELF OUT THERE 88

YOUR CHEMISTRY - CAN YOU DO THE WORK HERE WITH US? .. 92

- INTERPERSONAL SOFT SKILLS 92
- INTERVIEW RESEARCH 95
- INTERVIEW DAY CHECKLIST 96
- CLOSING THE INTERVIEW 98

KEEP CALM AND CARRY ON 104

- REVIEW, RESEARCH, REPEAT 107
- EXPAND YOUR SEARCH 107
- CULTIVATE LEADS 108
- THE NEXT OPPORTUNITY TO TALK 109

TRANSITION TO NEW ROLE 112

- NEGOTIATING WITH OFFERS 112
- CLARIFICATIONS NEEDED 113
- KEEP YOUR SEARCH UP 114
- MANAGE OFFERS AND ENQUIRIES 116
- MAINTAIN YOUR NETWORK 116
- KEEP UP WITH THE INDUSTRY 118
- STARTING OFF WELL 120

EPILOGUE 124

- CLOSING COMMENTS 124
- PERSONAL NARRATIVE 127
- INSPIRATIONAL SPEECH 131
  - STEVE JOBS 131
  - JK ROWLING 131

AUTHOR'S BIO 134

AFTERWORD 136

ACKNOWLEDGEMENTS **138**
LIST OF CONTRIBUTORS **139**

1. ABOUT THE AUTHOR

About the Author

Who I Am

I have a research and development sort of personality, so when I was a kid, I always wanted to find out how things worked. I had a curious nature and could simplify complex things. Also, I was always looking at any technology, especially when new things came out. Growing up in the eighties, there were things like the Walkman, Laserdiscs, VCR's that sort of thing.

I always wanted to find out how things were working on the backend, inside the machine. We used to find household appliances that people had left for scrap or something like that; a friend and I would strip it down using tools and unscrew it all and then see where all the pipes went and what the different mechanisms did inside. It was literally just to find out what was inside it and how it all fitted together. I guess things have changed now, but when I was growing up, many things were hardware-based. So, it was tangible, physical things that you could pull apart. It was mostly sort of dabbling; I grew up in a single-parent household, so I had to take it upon myself to solve these things. To investigate and find out myself how these devices worked, a journey of self-exploration in a way.

As well as messing with random scrap appliances, I also had the same mindset with early computers as well. I found them fascinating; I had an Amstrad CPC464, which was a really old computer game system, one of the first home PC and video games units. It had a really basic command line coding function, so even at an early age of eight years old, with one of the first computer systems launched, I was able to make a little game where a man could run across the screen, and that's just by reading through the manuals and trying stuff out in my own time. It was different when my friends came over, we would just play the video games, but when I was left to my own devices, I found this command line function within it, then read a little bit about it and was able to make a basic animation game.

Another friend at junior school had a BBC computer (which was the most sought-after machine in that period), as his father was a musician or sound engineer. He showed us a menu called 'edit6', so we were able to edit the system file. For us, it was really risky and a thrill to be coding at the system level, not like making a novelty animation. That was the first time that I saw you could actually go a little bit deeper and do things at a more fundamental level.

Throughout my childhood, I was an avid film watcher, so I was watching all the James Bond films and planning all the movies at Christmas. Watching those live Saturday morning kids programmes, I would set alarms for and did not miss any of the shows. That may have been the first indication that I was destined for the broadcast media industry. Who knew that I would later be doing this in enterprise-level broadcast systems and putting channels on-air.

Around the same period, myself and a friend were doing mix tapes, recording radio shows, and copying audio cassette tapes where you have two decks on a 'stereo.' We were able to cut and sample different sound bites to make new tapes, it was mainly just funny stuff, but it instilled in me this sort of passion of mine for using hardware to manipulate the media and the content – making something new out of something that's already existing.

As a school kid, I only enjoyed the social side to it and the academic side just developed from me doing as best I could and excelling in certain subjects. Always last minute with homework and deadlines, but there was a fine line between having too much of a good time and buckling down. But as many classmates left for the workplace, I definitely wanted to stick to the learning and carry on in the academic world. My parents didn't push me in any particular direction, and they would support me in whichever choices I made – this was good for me to choose my own path.

Thinking of the trends over my life it's tended to have switched between periods of learning and working, with gaining academic and professional qualifications in the learning periods it then propelled me to then excel further in the workplace. But I developed this skill of thinking laterally or alternatively and choosing a plan that not everyone else was following. One of them was to apply to University with actual grades not predicted and take a year out working and going to University when you're 19 and not 18 years old. Then things started to evolve from there, and I just started to notice things that took my interest and made me change direction to home in on more of the things that I wanted to do. So, when moving to the city in freshers' week, it was a massive upheaval for me (and my family letting me go), but it was a new and exciting time with like-minded people. I needed guidance with my pre-University aspirations so during those years at Leeds I'd follow instinct whether that's overheard snippets of conversation, things I noticed visually, butterfly feelings in your gut or just positive connections with people. Taking a gap year wasn't what normal course mates did, but it felt like the right move, so I took an opportunity, and it was like a big chess move for me at the time.

I got bitten by the travel bug after leaving university and to this day believe that my people skills developed hugely after travelling so much. I was dealing with so many different people and cultures, and often got dropped into a situation where I landed in a rural village and had to figure it all out. So, I got to be personable, friendly, flexible, calm, confident, and outgoing – this is all great practice on your interpersonal skills.

It's definitely a sweet spot with hard skills. One of my best traits is being able to bridge people and technology and being the conduit for that. So right now, I'm not at this detailed low level in terms of complex technology or coding, being a principal or senior engineer. I've figured out I don't really want to be, but I've got enough grounding in technology to match it with the soft skills and the people skills. That's just been a development over 15 or 20 years of basically fusing it together.

How I got here

My broadcast journey started in childhood, really looking at recording equipment, VCRs, cassette tapes, that sort of thing. I had a keen interest in making sure whenever I recorded a film, the commercials were not recorded. I used to be able to tell when the commercial adverts were coming up, as it used to have a moving stripe, which I found out later in life were called 'cue dots.' When I saw this chevron in the top corner, it was to signify a break was coming up, and I needed to jump out of my seat and press pause on the VCR top loader. When the commercials were ending, I would resume the recording, so the playback was seamless. So, whenever my family or myself wanted to watch the film again, they could watch it without any commercials because I'd literally edited them out of the recording as it was broadcasted live!

That was one of the most definitive early signposts but adding to this was going through junior school in the late 80's, I was a 'computer monitor' for a few years, which gave me an official-sounding title (and certificate). Basically, it was making sure all the computers were brought out of the storage room, plugged in and set up for use throughout the day, and then returned. In high school in the early '90s, I took subjects like 'Information Systems' on an Apple Macintosh and Business Studies lessons to learn about companies, investment, accounting, etc. (and using printers!). It raised a flag telling me that I should be learning this stuff, as I was interested in it. It felt like I was already on the right path, so I made sure I attended all those lessons and immersed myself in them, even though some of them were very dry.

After gaining 10 GCSEs in high school, I secured a place at the local college and chose three topics – Media Studies, Information Technology, and Geography. So, I definitely know that Geography is where the traveller inside me comes from and have managed to put it to good use! But the other two subjects at college were fundamental in fusing the media and technology education that I needed. It's interesting to recall my spare time at college, where I was always editing music videos above and beyond the course curriculum; it was just something that I wanted to do. Using the linear machines called assemble edit machines to do it shot by shot in sequential order. It was very manual, very hardware-based, but it was quite fun actually – you had to stripe the tape black, use the jog controls, set the in & out points, and as they were tape to tape, there was no room for error but the only edit suites available at the time. Online non-linear editing suites used to be all theory, as they were so expensive, so seeing the first software versions at University was quite radical.

When my college courses came to an end, I was deciding my next move during the summer of 1997; I was asking my Media Studies lecturers if they had any suggestions on possible options. "Well, Ben, we've heard this 'Multimedia Technology' is quite interesting to get into and might be the next big thing." I wasn't sure what to do at University. I'd done Media Studies but didn't really want to be a journalist or work with newspapers. I started looking into those courses; I saw some in Plymouth, in Salford Manchester, some up North in Leeds. But I decided to take a year's break anyway, so at that point, I just worked for a sports shop part-time, so I had enough money to sort of tide me over and save a little bit over a year for the following September. Instead of relying on predicted results, I had actual results, so I finished the course in the summer, got an unconditional place based on my results, and went to university a year later in September.

Having that sort of recommendation from my college lecturers spurred me on, and I ended up getting in a 'Multimedia Technology' undergraduate degree course. I started University in 1998 at Leeds Metropolitan. I can remember going up for an intake day, like an open day, and meeting tutors, seeing the labs were exciting; even the train journey was building anticipation.

The open day gave me a good insight into what media courses were offered in the department. It was a faculty Information and Engineering Systems (IES) at the time. But it just started doing Multimedia, so they were showing 3D modelling. That was the first time I'd ever seen 3D modelling with 3D Studio Max and stock kettle models rotating. It really opened my eyes to other parts of multimedia, not necessarily straight-up video (which is what I'd been used to) but also showing me all the sound booths and the School of Music. It was a great day, and I definitely felt at that point that I had made the right decision, so I got ready for university life.

In my Manchester social bubble, I had a great bunch of friends, we tried to go to as many gigs and concerts as possible; this unbeknownst to me was also a flag indicating the direction that I'd take. The best example was a Prodigy concert in the late nineties at Manchester Apollo where they had this Dutch VJ (video jockey) called Eboman. His style was video sample madness, being able to match images and video to what was happening with the sound. I just thought that's the sort of thing I wouldn't mind getting into. Most times, at gigs, I would be transfixed by the projection screens or video installations, which gave me some inspiration as well. I wondered, "How did they do that?" and once I have that thought in my mind, I like to get to the bottom of things and find out how they did it or to even reach out to them themselves.

In September 1998, I moved to Leeds. I was in halls for a year, made some great connections there, and I was getting inspiration starting from day one. I started meeting graphic designers, media course mates, editors, events managers, people involved in music technology, promoters, and even coders. So, it wasn't long 'til I started doing my own VJ gigs, fulfilling some dreams and actualizing some goals that I'd set subconsciously only a year earlier watching Eboman.

It was by making some links early on within the first year that gave me my first foray into networking and getting some connections in the live event industry. I'd figured out the software I needed to do these live events, so I started putting my services out there, doing some gigs, and getting paid for it—it was a very dynamic time. All this whilst studying Multimedia, experimenting with video samples out at night at live events that were shaping me through the early years at university. The course gave us some choices in the modules taken, so I focused more on interactive videos, like scripting, DVD authoring and also motion graphics, video editing, and some 3D. I did a final year project in 2002 on VJing and wrote a thesis on remote Video Jockey where instead of running a wire from building to building, you can do it through streaming video networks using a client and server. A visual artist sitting in the studio or even at home could work remotely and do visual projections at a live event with sound and audience present—however, internet (and early 2000 'broadband') connection is still required!

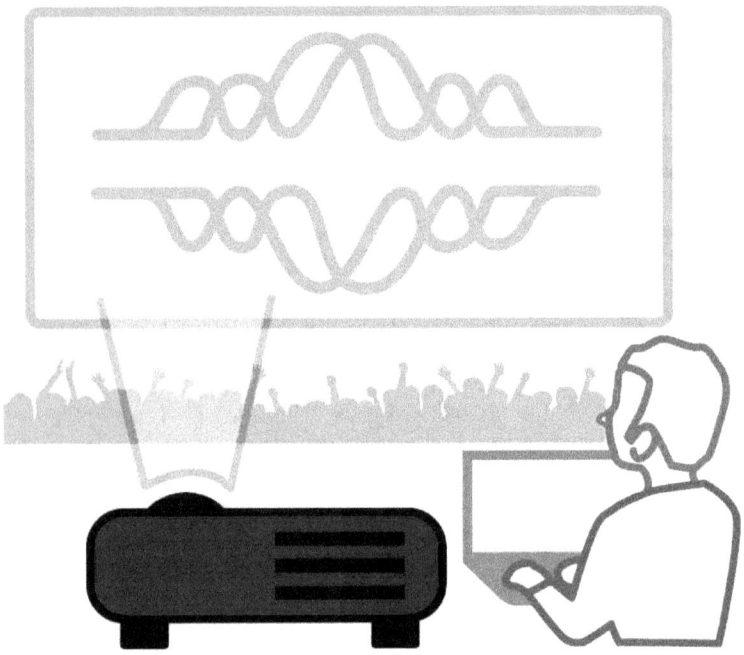

It was ahead of its time in many senses, especially with this entire home working going on now in the COVID-19 pandemic.

Another thing I did was to extend the course by a year and take a gap year on year three. So the three-year course became a four-year course with what they called a sandwich year in between. I made some good choices, as I needed to be fully immersed in the University environment and the way of life that it had, not only socially but my ever-growing VJ performances. I had some gigs booked at the university, and I was able to borrow some equipment, like projectors, and use it for the events at the union, so it worked well in that sense. During that gap year, I worked in the same Multimedia department I studied, who knew I'd be employed at Leeds Metropolitan University where I was a student. However, this is where I viewed it as an opportunity and was dealing with all sorts of media technology kit and computer administration at the time, figuring out how to use it and running training sessions on it.

So being on the other side of the Multimedia helpdesk counter, I was serving students who needed help with their Multimedia technology kit, basically with all the software, and some course mates were now finishing their 3rd and final year. It was a really big learning curve being in the workplace, employed full-time, as it instilled that work ethic again. So I'd flipped back to being in work mode. It was a nine-to-five job, and I knew I'd also have to flip back to academic mode on completion. It prepared me very well for the third year because I was up and ready at the computer at 9 am every day; it put some discipline in me, and I noticed the same when I spoke with others returning from their working gap years.

Always thinking alternatively or differently to the masses is a main theme of how I operate, not everyone does a gap year - it's low paid but it was crucial choice and one of those dots I could connect looking backwards. They must have thought highly of my work to keep me on right until the start of the next academic year, so instead of the year being 12 months, they extended it to almost 14 months.

Upon completing my final year, I passed the course with a 2:1, which I thought was a good result. There were only a handful of people getting a first; it was very difficult to achieve something like an 85% pass rate. But I was proud of my result in Multimedia Technology and so graduated in June 2002, then started looking for jobs over the summer. I got interviews with some of the types of companies I had in mind in the youth music industry. I got close with my idols at the time, Drum & Bass Arena, with their event web streaming, but the position didn't go ahead. Nevertheless, that didn't faze me, as I still had my own freelance work in Leeds. I was building up some more clients like councils, NGOs, and charities, so I had a pipeline of work at this point. Then looking to the future, I thought I needed to preserve this somehow. Not the status quo, but to keep this work going. It got to the end of summer, and I didn't have any offers for full-time work, but I did have some client work, so I needed to build my client base a little bit more.

At that point in late summer, I applied for the Master's (MSc) in Creative Technology at the same university. I had to take the hit and pay the tuition fees, but I decided to do that over two years, so it would lighten the load to pay it off gradually. It was kind of a tough time then to make this investment myself, as I had a limited client base, but I made it work and just pushed forward, as I thought this was the right way to go. Those two years were probably one of the most rewarding times of my academic student life. It was a close-knit group of 20 postgraduate students, everyone knew each other, and everyone was working with each other at any given point. We all kind of socialized together, we all did projects together, and you could tell where people's strengths lay with the projects they were producing. That's the point where I made the most long-lasting academic friendships from my student days. Most, if not all, of those friendships last to this day. Since then, we've been referring freelance work to each other, which is a testament to the quality of work and gathering for social occasions and shows the strength of bonds we made.

We finished the Creative Technology Master's postgraduate degree in summer 2004 and graduated in November. I had managed to gain and retain quite a few clients throughout my now six university years; I had now left the safety bubble and run out of academic road in that sense. So with more work still coming in, I managed to continue to be self-employed, working in multimedia, getting more freelance work in video editing and DVD authoring, and some web streaming work.

I'd had thoughts, visions, and ideas about making a move out of the city, but I ended up staying in Leeds, where my client base was, and started getting more interested in broadcast. Through mutual freelance work with friends of the MSc course, I did a few pieces of work to do with projections and cinema and started using a kit like a Mac Pro. Some had quite well-developed studios to work in (although home-based, they were separate rooms). It really switched me on to all the higher enterprise or professional levels of media technology, like all the companies in London would be using and all the professional galleries and studios use in the local area.

I'd joined 'incubator' schemes, tried council-run workshops, attended networking events at a new hip 'Round Foundry' for startup media companies, but I wasn't there and was stuck at home with a steady but limited client base. I needed to break this impasse of sorts, so in early 2006, I started working for an independent TV and Film production company based in Leeds, doing business development. That's where I started working more on my soft skills, going to all the networking events, started developing the people side more rather than the technology side.

It was the sales side that put me off, and as I'd had those thoughts earlier, my gut said—you need to make a bold move. I decided to take some time off to go travelling, I needed a break from it, and many university friends had done it anyway. I'd spent a couple of years after university doing freelance, and now I needed to switch things up or reinvent myself; this presented an opportunity to do that. In late 2006, I packed up my Leeds life and took six months off travelling around the world—full circle, covering most of the continents. I've always liked culture in general and to experience that all over the world was very appealing. I had a friend who had moved out to South Africa, so I figured I could head there first and meet up with him, setting me on my travelling adventure.

From a personal development point of view, having that six months gave me a chance to reflect and come back with a different mindset. I went all the way around Southern Africa, Southeast Asia, Australia, New Zealand, through the Pacific, and California before heading back to the UK.

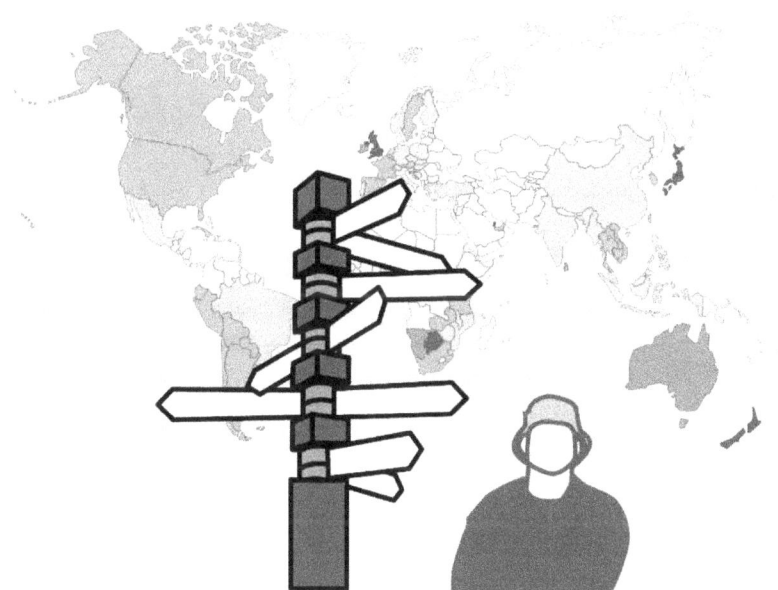

Those travel highs were met with flying lows back over the Manchester skyline on a cold, wet February night to my new reality. I had moved back 'home' and had to recalibrate myself to living back in my hometown, at the house I grew up in with zero money. I'd just gotten back and started to get some gigs back over the border in Leeds with old VJ contacts, and some old school friends had started getting involved with new promoters in Manchester. They were doing events for thousands of people at a time in Ape at Apollo, Northern Devolution at Roadhouse, and Warehouse Project at Store Street, where they had managed to get onto the video projection side of things.

They asked me to come down and do some VJ work with them, and these were weekly gigs. So already, I'd gotten myself straight back in it, started getting some new clients, and just started building up the client base again from where I'd left off, so to speak. It was either at live events, doing VJ performances or postproduction work in the home studio again. It suited me, as I could work on the post-production stuff during the week and the live event stuff a few evenings. So slowly but surely, over the course of 2007, I started building up my portfolio again and had quite a bit to show for it by the end of the year with other new festivals and fashion show gigs as well.

It was early 2008, and there was perhaps some higher purpose at play; there was something calling me essentially, I didn't know what it was at first. I started going to some technology trade shows, and I'd gone down to London a few times to some of these broadcast exhibitions specifically. I'd started focusing on IPTV and the head end of TV transmission in particular—it was something to aim for, at least. So I started buying some Cisco routers, I'd speak to some learning providers, and they'd tell me, "You won't be able to self-study all of this. You need the routers, as you need in-person instruction."

I kind of ignored the hard sell and said to myself, "You can do this on your own—have faith in yourself."

The Cisco exams have quite high pass rates at 85%, but I didn't let that phase me, as I had time on my hands at that point. I just self-studied the Cisco certifications, buying some quite thick, heavy books and tons of printouts. The dining room looked a bit like a computer room with all these routers in there and pages and pages of notes and diagrams! It was something to aim for, a little bit of focus. It was almost like an exit strategy at that point to be independent and in what I thought of as 'broadcast.'

So I set a date for the exam in my diary, and I always remember this day, I was still doing some client work, and was studying in the background around it. The exam was in Leeds, so I went over on the train, and when I got there 30 minutes early, the exam proctor asked for my passport (that I didn't have). I'd forgotten to bring it with me, so they said, "Well, you can't start the exam without us seeing a copy of it." I had to think laterally and quickly. I went into my bank, as they might have a copy of it, but they didn't. In the end, I had to ring up my mother and ask her to scan the passport and email it to me. It was probably the most difficult part of the day, but I guided her through putting the passport on the scanner, opening the software, scanning the passport in, and then emailing it to me as well. Oh, and all of this was on dial-up as well, which probably didn't help. She even emailed it to a lady called Barbara, a family friend instead of me (Ben).

But eventually, it came through with the scanned attachment, and I just forwarded the email to the proctor, and she printed out and accepted it. The problem was, she said, "You can start the exam now, it's 20 minutes in, but you'll have to finish at the same time as everybody else." So that focused the mind a little bit! I had to quickly go through the questions even faster than everybody else, without a chance to review or reflect on my answers much. But I managed to make my way through all the questions and do the final one by the time the finishing signal was going off. You find out the results then and there, and she said, "Well, congratulations, you got 86%. So, you've passed the exam." Obviously, I was ecstatic; it was a rollercoaster day, but then I felt almost invincible.

I wanted to pass the exam anyway, but it was even more incredible under the circumstances of the day. That's one of the reasons why I kept it on my CV, aside from being one of the best professional qualifications, I kept it on there even when it expired, as it provided a great interview story.

The financial crash of 2008 was in full flow, and there was not much work around anywhere. I was really struggling at that point in general; there was debt, bills, and bleak job prospects—basically, there was pressure. I applied further afield, and one of the only jobs in London that I applied for was at a digital playout centre in the City of London, and they asked me down for an interview. So I got up early, took the day return coach, and arrived early for the interview, which went OK, nothing to report back on, really. The channels were computer games, health and fitness, and adult at night—but it was great to see all the kits in the rack room, and it stirred my interest. I didn't hear back from them for a few weeks, but eventually, three weeks later, they called and said, "We'd like to offer you the job."

So I inquired, "Why the delay?" They said the other candidate had declined it, and as there were no other offers on the table from anywhere else, I decided to take it and move to London. That was in May of 2008, just as the global financial meltdown was in full swing, but I was fortunate to have work, I guess. It was shift work, either three or five days a week over the course of 14 days (the broadcast fortnight as it's known), so you do seven days of work at 12 hours a shift. Then I made London my home. I had a shared flat in East London which was within walking distance to work. I then started to make my way through London's professional broadcast industry. It was a small niche broadcaster, but I had to start somewhere.

I tried a subtle promotion and pay rise move, but it didn't come off, so I plotted an exit by moving from these basic channels to a multi-client service provider called Arqiva. They poached me on Facebook weirdly; they noticed my job title searching through and just messaged me. They'd been on my radar anyway because looking back, I actually worked with them on an outside broadcast for the Bollywood Awards a year earlier—so already there were some dots connecting for me. It was a step up, and in the right direction, it was an increase in salary as well, so a good opportunity to earn a little bit more. So as I moved jobs, I also moved flats to North London, as I had a cousin there. It was nice to be near some family and have a nicer flat as well. I was on the right side of London to commute to the new playout site, and with the new flat, my standard of life was improving in general.

The journey at Arqiva progressed from some server-based channels, basic shopping channels, and stuff like that to being promoted onto the ESPN live sports channels. I could hear the buzz of that new playout suite and felt the vibrant energy—they had everything, the premier league, FA cup, all the American sports, Monday night football, American football, ice hockey, and NBA basketball. That's where I really started learning about broadcast. It was such a dynamic place to work, everyone had to be on top of their game, as the service levels and expectations were very high. So again, starting at the bottom, I worked my way from the basic 'Classic' server channels of ESPN, then onto the live channels, mastered the network control (the small MCR), got to run the live ingest desk, and eventually shift leading as well, so supervisor of the whole shift. I really excelled at that point, making strides in many different ways in my career, so I volunteered to be on the employee representation forum, the representative for all the studios and playout suites, so I started to make some connections around the business in different teams, departments and senior management and still retain them to this day. I guess every good thing must come to an end, and in 2012 ESPN lost the Premier League rights, then the writing was on the wall for those channels to finish in their current capacity. In 2013, ESPN pulled out of the broadcast market in the UK, to which BT Sport took over the playout operations. At that point, I had to decide whether to carry on as 'normal' and perhaps do the same thing with BT Sport, or do I move on at this point and the situation presented itself.

I chose to move on. It took me a while, maybe a couple of months of reflection, to grasp the fact that I should move on and take the risk, plus there was a good financial package to provide a springboard into something new. If I was brave enough, made enough connections, had enough drive, and a strong enough CV and experience, then why not? It was sad to go, bittersweet in a way, but it was a really exciting time as well. I had some prototypes that I'd started developing at the same time, like the transmission outage simulator, some of the non-linear DVD authoring prototypes, and I had some good ideas that I could explore in a startup capacity.

I had quite a lot of connections on LinkedIn at that time, and there was quite a lot of support as well. So other people who were exiting the business were getting jobs elsewhere. Even as I was leaving, I was lining up interviews with other broadcast companies and service providers. I felt there was a place for me in the industry, either self-employed or full-time. So I left Arqiva in October of 2013, started getting some freelance work later that year, and started building up the 'Ancast' brand at that point—I had to decide a name quickly, and that seemed to roll off the tongue.

I started getting some branding, started giving out cards, had managed to make a basic website. In the new year, with some of the work I was going for, the recruiter said I needed to be a limited company. So I said, "Well, I've already got Ancast here ready." What they meant was I needed to be a properly setup broadcast contractor, so you're a business providing services rather than being a potential full-time employee—that was a flag that I was destined for self-employment next. The interviews were gathering pace; I had so many interviews with Globecast, Red Bee, Evertz, Grass Valley, each one improving with my preparation and interview style.

Then as so often happens, you get a call out of the blue, mine was in January 2014. My old manager phoned me up and said, "You know, I understand you've got a bit of work now, but are you going to be free for a potential project in Hong Kong soon?" I said, of course. I was setting up as a contractor with a registered business, which seemed to be another bonus for them. So they got me in for a kick-off meeting in the UK office, explained the objectives, and I was to start at the end of January through March over there. In a heartbeat, I took the opportunity to move out to the Far East for a few months doing what I loved—working with people and broadcast technology. I ran a project doing some beta testing for a cloud playout product. It was really like a prototype, so we had the hardware delivered and got everything set up. I had a small team of engineers and operators but worked with the Director of Technology as liaison for the client—Turner APAC. So after we got it set up and pulled together a test plan, I gave regular feedback to the management and to the manufacturer. I wrapped up the project there, handed in a final report, and came back to the UK but then a couple of weeks later got another contractor gig—I was in demand!

It just started progressing from there; I didn't really have much downtime after that, as the gigs kept coming, either consultancy or straight-up broadcast contractor. This continued on from 2014 and the years since I'd always have a new major client every year and have some time off in the winter. I'd try and finish a project in December or January and then have a couple of months off to travel and reset myself, coming back fresh to start on new projects in March or April. Then just repeated year after year doing the same thing, it really worked for me by rewarding myself with a few months of travelling and some downtime, then having some major, major projects to deliver for new clients when I came back. In 2017, I started diversifying and picked up some lecturing work, again with a previous contact, doing some seminars at Ravensbourne University in Greenwich.

From that year on, I started concentrating more on developing Ancast a bit further as well. I like to keep busy anyway so to strengthen my credentials I had a couple of relevant professional qualifications in mind and noted I had a few weeks gap before my next gig. I'd use that time wisely and do a scrum master course, or I'd do an ITIL service management course, or I'd do a business analyst course—anything that adds value to the brand. It's always good to add to the CV and make sure you're on top of the professional certifications. I also began overhauling the website, doing the podcasts, articles, posts, etc. That's where I've ended up today; actually, this is how I've got here essentially. I always have my diary full of things to do because to me, I just treat every day as the job, no matter whether it's onsite with a client or whether it's developing my own business and my own brand. Just generally being driven and proactive, meeting people for lunch, trade show, that sort of thing. We've all ended up in late 2020 with a lot of time to reflect during the pandemic, a lot of homeworking, and looking back in a retrospective way, and so that made me think of writing this book too.

Why Write a Book?

After some reflection over the past year in the coronavirus pandemic and wanting to, how I phrase it, 'pay it forwards,' I wrote this book. It's like giving something back almost, I can appreciate how fortunate or lucky I am, so I want to impart it to others. Sometimes you make your own luck, but I feel like I need to give something back to the people who were in my position many years ago. Not just the skillset and discipline, but also wanting to share my experience and even if it led to giving somebody, somewhere, the edge one time. So, I like to include all the insights I can give and 'The Inside Track' of podcast excerpts from guests sharing their stories. I guess it's those little nuggets of information or recounting a time and a place where something profound happened, something that changed the course of my career or caused a flag, that are important to recount. Looking back these tend to be the highlights of your career and at the time I've often thought to myself 'this is just awesome, you'll remember this forever' - kind of imprinted on your brain.

As the years pass, I have achieved quite a lot, especially since moving to London, and I guess I didn't always know what I was going to do. For a lot of people that would be in the same position where they have a broad landing zone. They have an umbrella or category they associate themselves with, but not necessarily a niche job role or job title, perhaps. Having gone through a few different broadcast companies, seen the academic side from both study and teaching about the industry, I want to essentially pass on my journey. It might ring true for readers, who also find themselves in a similar situation. It's to help give them a bit of confidence that what they are doing is the right thing, there are other people going through this, and there's light at the end of the tunnel.

You might think it's a waste of time doing certain things or could be looking for a bit of inspiration as well, really. I've achieved a few of my dreams from self-actualization, where I move on from one thing to another to try and master a new role, skill, and craft. I guess now, aside from moving into some new areas of broadcast technology for me, this is one of the things I need to be content with—the giving back. Passing on insider knowledge to anyone who finds it useful, hence why I'm writing the book. There's a trail of dots that I've left through my career, and hopefully going to look back and join them up.

I was once where you are now, and I'm trying to instil that confidence in you that the journey you're about to go on is quite exciting, and it can turn many corners. Although you are not sure what you're looking for, you'll know exactly what it is when it comes across and presents itself. And remember not to dwell too much on decisions, as any taken were the right decision at that time.

So pause for thought and think how far are you into your broadcast media journey and what can you do now to change your career trajectory?

2. INTRODUCTION

Introduction

Perhaps it's early in your career search, and you are wondering how on earth you can get from zero to hero in the brave new world of broadcast media. You have an idea of what you want to do but a daunting feeling of how you are going to get there–don't worry, this is natural. There may be times when you are fed up with trying to find where relevant jobs are posted, wonder what the point is in going to an event, or maybe a low 'rate of return' when you fill in countless online applications. It can be like you're stuck in a rut, in an endless cycle of sending your CV off unedited to as many people or companies you think will work on a 'hit and hope' scattergun strategy. This coupled with the odd email about unadvertised jobs to somewhere on your radar in the hope you can 'bypass' normal channels and get in through the side door–but the reply and all other automated ones, are essentially rejection ones.

In this book, I write about how individuals with little direction or those with clear goals have a successful entrance into the industry. It takes you through the industry landscape and then focuses on your values and how they will make you shine to those potential hirers. This is where you need to take stock, focus on getting where you want to be, and treat your career search like a full-time job. The fundamentals are all about competency, compatibility, and chemistry for you to do the role at their company with the people there. By going through these sections, finding out more about yourself and the industry, is going to give you better preparation for the main event–the interview. It doesn't stop there. With the guidance here, you can use your soft skills to shine. Even if successful, the book will also give you insight into maintaining and progressing your career in broadcast further.

This might sound easier said than done, but take it from me, I have been in a similar situation like the global pandemic. Take the financial crash of 2008, with freelance and full-time broadcast media jobs becoming scarce, money was becoming tight, and I was embarking upon this search - well, I used what I lay out here in the book to get into it. The book is not only from my personal experience of getting these roles but also the workshops and courses I've had throughout my career, and I can help you to do the same.

Coming from an academic background in creative technology, I've spent many years doing work such as programmer, web design, live animation graphics, video editing, DVD authoring, production filming, post-production effects, to name a few disciplines. Then comes the technical and broadcast experience of engineering, IP networks, project management, TV channel playout, media management, and workflow to recently being an all-rounder consultant–there isn't much I've not experienced. The book is a great introduction to the industry at a high level for those who might not want to follow their chosen academic course outcomes or know what job they actually want. There are so many industry roles, both agnostic and specific, that by finding out more about the broadcast media ecosystem, you might even feel it changes what you thought you were looking for by knowing more about your values.

Once you have set up your 'framework' for your career search, you always have something to go back on, to work on, to read up on, and another step to get you there. Done right, you will be in a position where dealing with your search gets easier due to the work you put into it early on; this will cut out the hit and hope strategy and get you focused on the good stuff. In that 2008 crash, I got some Cisco networking certificates (from self-studying), as I wanted more 'technical' full-time roles. I was unexpectedly offered a role in London, but for a more senior role—I felt the hard search work had paid off. Even now, in recent times, I know by heart, my own strengths, motivations, values, and skills (such as CV writing) that I can use to get in front of hiring managers more easily. Once I'm interviewed, the soft skills kick in, and I use my industry knowledge in a position I know I can fulfil. I'm often seen as an SME (subject matter expert)—even in a position where terms cannot be agreed, the tone remains cordial, keeping them in my network going forwards.

If there is only one thing that you take away from this book is that you will feel that you are the better candidate for your broadcast media role applications. With all the detail on making your search successful, it will make you a lot more comfortable in interviews, positive and conveying an air of assertive confidence that you are the right pick for the job. So when do you feel like taking this search by the horn? The answer is right now—by the time you finish the book, you will be ready to do your search the right way and with urgency. The quicker you change your attitude and the way you approach the task at hand, you should be one step ahead of the rest and 'get to work' on it. You are the only one in charge of your career—no one else and do remember that; I wish you the very best in getting what you want out of your career in this wonderful industry. So please read on; you will find you learn something new and get industry insider tips that will enable you to get to your career destination a lot quicker.

Identifying the Problem

Think of Einstein's famous quote, *"Insanity is doing the same thing over and over again and expecting different results."* If all you have done is visit on one website and clicked submit to all new jobs with the same CV, then this might be an Einstein moment; if you just ring one recruiter every week and you're not having any luck, this might be another Einstein. The first instinct for newcomers is either to have the scattergun approach and a kind of hit 'n' hope tactic or the opposite extreme where you think something will just come along. In the first place, graduating from a course or coming of working age and wanting just to get into the industry, you still have to get in front of hiring managers, so just having one strategy or none at all will not put you in a strong position being a candidate.

Another key problem is not knowing what you want to do yet, you have perhaps graduated or have been in the same job role, and it's just not working for you. These are a bit more difficult to get to the bottom of, as it requires some self-reflecting instead of just switching tactics. In this sense of knowing what the problem is, by understanding what you do and don't like for a start. Look at the broadcast skills that you may have, which ones did you feel comfortable with or enjoyed doing and bore fruits in terms of output or qualifications—this might help you work it out.

I have experienced all of the above, so there is nothing out of the ordinary about it; it's just that you have to learn when this is a problem, so it's flagged to you and identified. In my early media days, leaving my undergraduate course, I tried some limited strategies and came close to landing a dream job in the summer break but only to return to studying. But then, even in the dizzy heights of working in live sports channel playout, such a dynamic place to work and where people would do anything to get a job there, I stayed in the same role for too long. Looking back, in hindsight, I should have stayed for 2 years max and moved on, but sometimes you get in a comfort zone, and it's always useful to recognize that.

This is taking a helicopter view of the broadcast media landscape, so I want to introduce you to the problem essentially. It's knowing your competency and leveraging your personal style. Or I want to phrase it as your personal brand, so this sits with your behaviours and personality. Knowing that, you try all the tools of the trade and then keep the best ones in your own toolbox from those that you're most comfortable with. The ones that you feel you can carry out with ease and not too much pressure. Something you are really excited to carry out.

Ancast Insight

Let me give you an example; I know I'm not a software developer, programmer, or coder, nor a principal engineer or senior broadcast engineer. I don't apply for these roles and actively deny I am such a person during the interviews. So if some job roles require some technical skills, then I won't profess that I'm a top-level engineer or a senior architect or that sort of thing. Just be honest with your own competency, really.

The worst position to land in is not being able to deliver if you have overstated your competency. When I was interviewing for Discovery, I'd describe myself as a 2.5 line engineer. It needed the experience of being the face of the project, which was perfect for me and the assignment at the time. I tried to project the image that I could get to grips with the technology, understand the terminology, and understand on a fundamental level what the engineering and technical infrastructure was all about. But that real low-level engineering detail is lost on me actually, so in this particular role, Discovery wanted a client-facing engineer. They already had quite a lot of third-line engineers and developers on the team that I was going to be embedded in. So I didn't try to compete with any of that. I leveraged my personal style, which is being a conduit between people and technology, and it worked.

Having explained that, I understood and got the technology, but equally, I had the soft skills as well to be in a client-facing role. It even shows on my CV as well; I just describe what my competencies are at the top, technical and personal. Then just being honest with the previous assignments and job roles that I've had. I'd listed things that I was more than comfortable with, broadcast systems that I was happy to manage on a technical level and was not trying to be anything more. The more you experiment and try out different competencies in the broadcast industry, you'll find the ones that you like and that suit your personal style the most anyway. Knowing your limits is definitely one of the best things to master in the broadcast industry, even from this high-level helicopter view.

Search Like it's a Job

This is where your work ethic shines through; being unemployed does not mean 9-5 has gone, and you have carte blanche to sleep in and read the papers all day. Think of it this way; the more effort you put into your 'working day,' the more you can count down to finishing 'work' aka doing your job search and then relaxing and having free time. My first time realizing this was during a sandwich year at university where I had to get up every day and be there for 9 AM no matter if I was still living in the student accommodations or not. This set me up well for my final year, where I quit my part-time job and for the final few months just wholly dedicated my working days to course work and graduating—and it worked.

But even if you're wanting to get in without formal qualifications, or perhaps you take the decision to move on from a role, and you have no new job secured, then this is where you need to 'work' for it. Is there somewhere you can go to not be working from your bedroom on your job search, even if it's a spare room, someone else's place, or even a cozy shed! It's the routine of it and the separation of your sanctuary of home that will help you focus and then switch off. Make sure you have stable internet; no distractions, and it has all you need for a day's 'work'—this includes where to have lunch and where you can break out.

It's productive, which is what you need, and I have done it every time I have to separate home life from the career stuff. I've used the university library before, as it was quiet, warm, had good internet and food and drinks places nearby—most of all free, so make use of it. But it doesn't stop there, thinking of my quiet periods in my career, I have managed to get free office space to work from, so I get up and cycle there to get my exercise at the same time—when I arrive, I'm pumped for the day ahead, getting my next broadcast role. I found free workspace offers even if they were time-limited; I used one for a week straight and then found another hot desking style place or even digital nomad/remote working style venues that can be suitable.

It could even be quiet cafes, but you'd have to pay and stock up on their coffee, obviously! Otherwise, just another room in your house that you can set up your stuff, as it's from all the above places that I have worked on my search, making contacts, filling my diary, doing applications, networking with people, developing my portfolio—these are your search tasks. I remember working at one of these fancy hot-desking workspaces, finishing my search week, I posted a picture up on Facebook—a mutual friend saw it and messaged me to say, "Come for Friday afternoon rooftop drinks." She worked in tech. There was some crossover with firewall products used in client broadcasters' infrastructure, so again, some networking with her colleagues! I left there about 6 pm Friday evening and got a call out of the blue from a recruiter, wanting to set up a next day phone interview for a broadcast architect role—this was linked to the search activities that I'd spent 9-5 all week doing.

Start simple with routines, make your bed in the morning, walk to the shop for your croissant, have something in your diary at 9 AM every day—it's all about structuring your day like a working day. This is where your calendar comes in handy; if you need focus time for working on your broadcast portfolio, CV, or online brand, then block it out in your week's grid. Things may take priority, so still keep them in but drag the blocks of time around, lengthen or shorten it accordingly —but the key thing is it will still get done! This is good practice for the broadcast world anyway, as everything moves so quickly, your diary is always on the move, so enjoy putting in meetings/calls with people, adding events, adjusting time set aside for search tasks.

And just as important as putting effort into the working week is the downtime too, just with any job, don't get burnt out by it. Make the most of the evening and weekends by not being stressed and anxious about your search as you have put the hours in all week—everyone needs to clock off for the weekend. Besides, most people are only around during the working week; emailing people outside of these hours won't get you much response, save it 'til they're in!

The key thing here is, it's not if, but when you'll get a job in the broadcast industry. It's notoriously difficult to get entry into the industry itself. The rate that jobs are applied for, especially on Guardian jobs, BBC jobs, that sort of thing, is high.

You could easily get hundreds of applications for one job opening, so it's a very competitive industry to get in, but not impossible. If you really want to get in the industry, then there are ways in, and I guess I'm a testament to that. A lot of my colleagues and people who are reading might find this rings true as well—treat the search like it's an office hours job in many senses.

Ancast Insight

Looking for specific examples, I had a quiet patch in my Ancast client work. I had just returned from a winter trip, travelling around Africa. I got back, and it coincided with finishing one accounting period in April, and then the idea was to hopefully start a new assignment when the new accounting year came in—but it took until mid-June to secure a new broadcast contract role.

So what did I do for two and a half months? Well, I got up every day and treated it like it was a full-time job. I launched my website, the first one I'd built myself; previous to that, I'd only had a domain forwarding into either a LinkedIn or a YouTube site or something like that. I used this time to make a custom company business website, completely overhauled my LinkedIn, made sure that it was separate from my CV, so they look completely different. I upgraded my email to the G Suite, so I was more productive. The small things like email signatures, making the email address first name dot last name—just made it look a bit more professional. I attended loads of trade shows at the time, around April, May, and June; there were one or two a week of different trade shows going on in London. Then interspersed were other events that were hosted at company offices, half-day workshops, or networking events. I was basically getting myself out there, and what clinched it was I started posting some updates on my social channels. I made a Facebook page, a Twitter handle, made the Ancast company profile on LinkedIn, and then started linking it together with a product called Hoot Suite.

I was posting updates from the trade shows, posting updates about the new website launch. Then a recruiter phoned me to confirm availability and asked, "Would you mind a phone interview on Saturday?" So, I had a half an hour call with the hirer who asked, "Can you come down on Monday to the office?" So I went down, spent maybe an hour in a face-to-face panel interview, and then they said, "Can you start on Tuesday?" It was to fill a solutions architect role that left me preparing a proof of concept for a customer demonstration at Encompass Digital Media in London. It was one of the companies that I wanted to do some contracting with; they were on my 'list,' so to speak. The project itself was great; it was an end-to-end IP video production demonstration. It came at the right time (my quiet period) and because I'd spent the previous two months just getting myself out there, getting my personal brand. It was off the back of something that seemed like it wasn't getting much traction or wasn't getting many views, then managed to pull something out of the bag.

This is why you should make sure you keep to a job search discipline and just make sure you can fill up your diary even though you don't have a job yet. Even if it's blocking out hours to do certain things like I was blocking out an hour every few days to organize some social media posts. With more attention, they would look professional when they got posted out. So even time boxing your diary, just to make sure you've got some focus time, otherwise, it fills up, but you have no time to complete the work tasks. People definitely notice, it's also building your portfolio at the same time, strengthening your own personal brand, and that's definitely a good thing.

Make a Promise

We are all guilty of procrastination to some extent; how many times have we all cleaned our rooms to put off doing some work? Or think about the broadcast media courses that you end up cramming for towards year-end, as you have literally put it all off throughout the semester, and now you finally have to deliver. Well, pressure does bring out the best in people, but it's much better to work ahead, as there are things that have lead times that you need to deliver anyway—-one of them is securing that job in the industry.

Everyone has an internal compass, their north star, or just guard rails, but it's important to have something to aim for and at least a broad landing zone. Don't try to solve everything at once, as you can only deal with what's in front of you, but by dividing the job search into manageable chunks, you can better manage your time and have achievable goals. This is important, as there's often too much 'noise' if it's just a wall of work to get through, and you need to treat finding your broadcast role as a job for now.

Start with the area of broadcast you want to get in and then work backwards, have some attending interview targets, applications applied for, emails to hiring managers, new contacts made, etc. These can just be numbers, but what you can also promise yourself is to dedicate time in your diary for developing online profiles, networking, updating versions of CVs, expanding your target matrix, and so on. All of this will more than fill your diary for the week, and when you fulfil your promise and you start reaping the rewards, it will be evident in the replies you get and the interviews you attend.

On the simpler side, it could well be that you promise yourself not to watch daytime TV, to get up at a set time, and only take 45 minutes for lunch, which is easily achievable. The key is not to over promise and under deliver, which is sometimes a problem in the real industry! But for candidates, it's good to understand what's realistic and still move forward in your broadcast career search. When you're starting out, it's understood by hiring managers that you don't bring the wealth of experience, so work on the things you can control. It may be to update a blog once a week, post something on LinkedIn, like or comment on so many items online a day—you never know where it may lead.

Some people make even higher promises, such as wanting to 'do international broadcast work' or 'get a detached house with a family,' which are then dreams to achieve. The more dreams you achieve, the more self-actualization can happen where you realize your full potential. Nonetheless, it will all start with making your way up the broadcast media ladder. In this level of goals, it's important to try to visualize what the ideal situation might be and then work back from there.

You have got to promise yourself; it's a call to action, basically—don't wait, otherwise, you'll be waiting forever. The solution is following a method that works for you and by reading the sections in the book to help you find them. Hirers are looking for solutions, so you have got to match them with the benefits you can bring—so what method can you use? The proof is written in the book, that's in the examples and the real-world insights that I can give you. They relate directly to how I have gone ahead, used certain techniques and useful ways to get ahead in the industry, and it pays dividends.

Why not choose now, this moment, today to change that mindset - what will it take for you to take on this challenge and ask yourself sincerely 'do I really want this?'

Ancast Insight

To give you a bit of firsthand experience of this when I was based at my home office (AKA, dining room table). I promised to build my online presence, and from there, started teasing out leads and opportunities. I had that sort of rigid timetable and was exploring all sorts of avenues to open things up. I was able to get some more traffic to the static website, so I started learning about analytics and understanding where in the world the website hits were coming from. I was gaining new knowledge from the trade shows, often I didn't go for a free lunch, but I would go to get some industry insight and some knowledge that nobody else had—that would be my gain. If I could do something that would mean me having the upper hand in interviews, then great. I'd be bumping into some existing contacts or meet some new ones who would give me further insights, not only on industry matters but also on what was happening within broadcast companies.

If I bumped into an old colleague, for example, then I might be able to get the inside info on what's happening in their place. It could be some new projects coming up, some movers and shakers within the company, some new technology going in. It all comes from what you can glean from these conversations over lunch, at after-work events, even for social drinks and networking occasions.

At that time, not only did one offer come through from Encompass, but at the same time, I just had Globecast, another broadcast service provider who was interviewing me too. I'd gone to the second interview round with them, as I had impressed them in the first interview. They got me back to speak with the deciding manager; I had just come from the Google Cloud Next trade show with a branded notebook and pen. The project was to roll out a global cloud project, and I just explained that I'd just come from the Google cloud show and told them all about my experience with cloud playout solutions and all my project work.

But to add to the search for work that was paying dividends, I also had BBC interviewing me at the same time for an internal consultant role. I spent two hours giving them a presentation with a brainwave alternative style with foam boards, printed photos, me pinning stuff on it, and kind of blew them away with it all. As I was leaving, I said, "You can have that if you want."

And their eyes lit up, saying, "Oh, thanks very much!" I was getting offers from all these companies, but I had to choose the one closest to my personal working style and not to play them off each other, really. So, I actually chose the Encompass one, as it was a solutions architect role—something I was keen to experience; it appealed to me more than the other two, to be honest. All of this is because I didn't wait. I took the call to action, "I need to do this, this, and this" every day and made some promises and made it a job for a while.

3. INDUSTRY LANDSCAPE

The Broadcast Media Landscape

Types of Roles

Many know what types of roles they want in the industry, others not so much, but generally, they roll up until into macro-level types.

The Inside Track

An excerpt from Ancast's podcast with Grace Amodeo giving her real-life insight.

Grace Amodeo: Well, the good thing about film school, like I said, is that you're surrounded by like-minded, creative filmmakers. So the big benefit there is that every weekend someone is making a film and they need people to help with that film. Usually, you don't get paid, but you're a student, so it's fine.

So what I ended up doing was, you know, I studied actually directing, even though I ended up in a production role, what I actually majored in was directing. So we had class projects and school projects, and just passion projects that people wanted to do on the weekends. So that's kind of how you get your start.

I mean, I remember getting hired as a key grip and a boom operator, and you know, when you're in film school, you kind of just say, "Hey, you, can you hold a microphone? Come on set and help me make this project". So you get to really experiment in a lot of different roles; I ended up realizing that producing and production was really where I wanted to be.

I don't think I had the creative drive that directors really need to have. I think what I really enjoyed about filmmaking was helping other people kind of facilitate their projects. So I was really good at making budgets and making spreadsheets and making call sheets and organizing all of the crew and making sure we had the permits.

That was kind of where I fell into realizing that producing was what I enjoyed doing. So I made those relationships in school and kind of kept those relationships through the years.

Ben Anchor: Yeah, that's interesting because a lot of people think, you know, it's all very sort of glamorous. They want to be near the cameras, but there's almost that producer side and almost like a project manager role, or I'm not going to say it's an admin role, but it's really important work, and it's not the first thing people think of, but it's crucially important, right?

Grace Amodeo: Very, very important. And it takes a certain personality type, you know, a very type, a kind of organized person. And for me, I think a lot of people that go to film school, like you said, they have this kind of magical idea about, you know, being Martin Scorsese and being Steven Spielberg and being the one behind the camera, calling the shots.

But you have to realize that on that film set there's 20, 30, 50 other people doing other jobs that are just as important. And if you can find that thing that you really like, and for me, I didn't mind not being the director and not being the person calling the shots. I really enjoyed, you know, helping in a different way and being the person that told everyone where to be, when to be there, here's who we need.

Here's how many people we need, here's how much money it's gonna cost, here's how we stay under budget, here's how we stay on time. I mean you can't make a film without that person, and I just found that that's the kind of work I liked doing.

'Broadcast Media: The Inside Track' Podcast published 15th March 2021 on various platforms.

Creative

The types of roles you'll typically find in production, post-production, studios, and those sorts of areas. For example, in some areas in London, particularly Soho, some parts of the east and west end and the studios further out of greater London, that's anything to do with filming and production. Those areas, especially central, tend to have creative agency talent in there too. Also, the print and digital broadcast journalism flourish there too.

Technical

There's the technical area that covers roles like engineers, broadcast IT, systems and workflow specialists, systems integrators, solutions architects, developers, and programmers, and those sorts of roles. They can be within a company with its own technical discipline, or you could even have technical people working for broadcast manufacturers or, more recently, cloud providers as well.

Operational

And then there are operations—this is what everything becomes in the end; if people aren't on projects and are keeping the channel ticking over, then this is it. Think of planning schedules on the channels, channel administration, channel marketing, content management, managing the programs delivery, the promotional placements, and the video-on-demand scheduling online. These are all making sure the operation is predictable with many roles carrying out the tried and tested processes and procedures. Making sure the linear channels are on air, the website has got all the content on it, and the platforms have got all the live channels and the on-demand services. It's making sure all those are running smoothly. Essentially these could be for broadcasters, service providers, or even manufacturers.

Commercial

There's an often-overlooked area that is commercial; these mainly deal in sales, so selling air time on the channel and perhaps selling new services. For broadcasters, it's creating ways to sell their advertising space via commercial content such as adverts, sponsorships, teleshopping, and partnerships. Service providers do the opposite and offer as a vendor to provide services to run the channel such as production companies, channel playout, video on demand, distribution, and media management. So their sales departments are always looking for tenders, bids, and add-on sales for existing clients. It's worth mentioning that typically the executive would be at the commercial level as well with a chief officer managing the company's finance department.

Project

Some of the other not-so-obvious roles in the industry are project roles; this is typically to deliver a change in how the company wants to operate over a period of time. Whereas those types listed above are more of an ongoing and steady state, the project roles will deliver change essentially and a bit more ad hoc. This could be working within a company's dedicated project management function or coming in on a contractor or consultant basis. Typical roles include project office, business analysis, technical delivery, architecture, engineering, and project or programme management if the change is on a large enough scale. Test management of broadcast solutions and also business change management are included as well, though slightly different from project management.

Ancast Insight

On my journey through broadcast, I've encountered most of these, so I will share some Ancast insights into that. Some readers may know what role they are destined for, some are in a transition period, and some need to try out a few disciplines. But when you find it, you'll know it.

On the creative side, I started out in the live events and post-production areas myself; I've naturally gone through quite a lot of these roles on my broadcast journey. It seemed natural to start doing VJ performances and filming live events, then moved onto video editing and authoring DVDs, or when I got a lucky break, I was part of a live outside broadcast in the 'Bollywood Awards' just after I left university. I thought that was going to be the pinnacle of my career; I thought that's where it all happened, basically wherever the cameras were. So wherever and whenever an event was live, that would be the end-all and be-all, but actually, after I went through a few of those different types of production jobs in the creative sector, I moved on. I mean, the hours didn't suit me; the VJ gigs and the filming gigs are typically at night or on the weekend.

I started to focus more on broadcast and having researched the salaries found were a decent amount in TV operations, then I started gearing myself up for that, to pull out of the purely creative area and go a bit more into technical operations. So in London, I worked my way up from entry-level niche broadcasters to known channels on a shift rota. Then at the top of my game in terms of TV operations were the ESPN live sports channels; it was probably one of the busiest TV operation centres I've ever worked in. We were running four live feeds all over the UK, Europe, and the Middle East, plus a live ingest desk with its own MCR. I was getting the best in terms of experience in TV operations. It was so dynamic, and everyone worked to the best they could. It was a great time, and I spent four amazing years learning how busy shift teams function, working with some great people, and really maximizing my operational experience.

Actually, as things progressed, I was instigating changes to improve the operation by introducing mini projects in it, giving direction to a developer to edit the schedules. I felt I'd exhausted this type of operational work, so I got some professional certifications, studied off my own back, made some connections, and at some point, I'd asked for a secondment in engineering; however, although this didn't materialize, it left me to concentrate on the project side. I was looking for any project courses to give me those skills and eventually got the qualifications needed. Since then, I've performed a few different types of roles, from management to engineering and some in between. Managed some small projects, have been involved in project engineering, and more recently, business analyst work and sort of found my passion.

Business Analysts (or BAs) can go quite deep on the technical level, but they've got to have those soft skills too. For me, it was being a conduit between people and technology, so I knew that way I could be on top of my own game, use my skill set, and sort of treat it like a hobby in many ways, to be honest. Trust your gut. It was the same as when I heard my lecturers at college tell me that they heard multimedia technology is good to get in. These flags and signposts were there, and I followed my instinct to find the discipline that I felt most comfortable with. There's nothing wrong with that; that's all part of the journey. You could make your way through a number of different types of roles and different areas of the media landscape along the way.

Types of Companies

You may not have thought about the place you do your broadcast work from, but it's often not working in a comfy chair out of a trendy office somewhere. In fact, starting out, you could possibly be working on small-scale collaborative projects with your acquaintances or simply continuing your search from home, but then get a call at any moment to offer you some work experience. When you're just starting out, then more or less any work offered in broadcast media, whether it's paid or if you want to volunteer for free, means you could be rocking up to a place you didn't envision. Nevertheless, if it gets you one step closer to your target role, then embrace it and experience a part of the industry.

We've all probably done some work together in each other's houses, for many people, this is their office anyway, especially in remote working times. But it's often the case where new starters in the industry often come across freelance work and need some help with the gig and enlist some of their network. It works both ways, so if by searching you find a gig, it would be likely that sometimes you'll need help too, so if it's not a shoot on location and you're trying to save money, you may well end up in someone's home studio or office.

But let's look at the bigger picture, as these small-scale broadcast gigs mean it will often suffice, especially if the client is happy with the work and the value it gives them from a cost perspective. But we all have aspirations, and it is a natural progression to move onto established broadcast companies and their production suites, high-rise offices, and city-centre locations. For example, you may be aiming your search for 'a small broadcaster, off-centre business park, recently established'—this is finding a niche but building up a picture of where you want to work. In this instance, it could be a cloud-based local news broadcaster who enjoys cheaper rent a few miles from the centre but has a station and vibrant food/drink courts which you can cycle to—that's the sort of thing to hone your search down if that's your thing and you saw a job crop up there, I'd say you'd be applying in an instant.

It's a given that the more well-known the broadcast company, the more difficult it is to get a foot in there with the prestige, scale of applications, and often central locations. Why not sidestep that and work your way up from a left-field option of getting similar work and getting promoted or going for less known companies and proving your worth there. Some of the factors that may influence the type of company you go for are the type of broadcast company, employee numbers, revenues, main location, if it has international offices, if your recruiters deal with them, and people who you know are there.

Broadcasters

Working for broadcasters, they are typically the rights holder, and it could be public service broadcasters or commercial broadcasters. They typically outsource a lot of their operations. From distribution and channel playout, for example, it's not a moneymaker; it's purely a cost, so they generally outsource quite a lot of their service providing aspects.

Public broadcasters tend to have the highest viewership. In the UK, they are in the 10's of millions. Therefore, any jobs come at a premium and any candidates of an exceptionally high standard. When speaking with the older generation of industry colleagues, they often regard the BBC as the university of broadcasting with thousands of applicants for as little as 20 cohorts taken on—with those not deemed up to scratch not making the grade. The public broadcasters tend to have the biggest infrastructures with their complicated online offerings, and regionalized TV output means their backend systems are a huge undertaking. Any productions and change projects tend to be well funded and come with a high level of governance, and corporate scrutiny as these have public service broadcasting remit.

Commercial broadcasters are the other large contingent where in terms of channel numbers far outweigh the public ones, and in terms of viewership, the American commercial broadcasters are the ones taking in the highest audiences, and therefore, revenues. Because they are numerous, it's likely you will see them posting vacancies often, as their primary goal is revenues over public service, and they tend to get resource gaps plugged quickly.

Service Providers

Then there are broadcast service providers; these actually provide outsourcing. These are typically multi-client, and they have a mixed technology stack to cope with each client's demands. It can be very, very dynamic because there's a high degree of change going on. There are quite a few service providers on the market. So they have to be on the sharp end of the client's requirements and demands. Well, I guess that's what makes it cutting edge at the same time.

A lot of these service provider names you may not have heard before, but you will quickly learn that they are a staple of the industry. They offer to handle services that broadcasters deem they cannot profit off of or that they are best handled by specialists who deal with unique service requirements better than they do—a great reason to work for them.

Content Providers

There are content providers in the broadcast media industry, so these could be what are also described as aggregators. Think of it as a middleman to receive content from; it could be some of the short-form commercials and interstitial providers. They will have two or three different aggregators to feed into, so the rest of the industry has only two or three places to go rather than hundreds or even thousands of different independent creative agencies or production houses. There are also distributors, so these are the big names. Your BBC Worldwides, Endemols—big studios, they sell a series at a time or a film deal, that sort of thing. And as well as that, there are some large, well-known post houses that deal with producing long and short-form commissioned content. A lot of post-production houses deal with taking the filming from the productions and putting it all together into the episodes, the films, or the short form promos and interstitials.

Production Companies

These can be independent production companies that carve out a specialist niche in the filming world and pull the cast, crew, and shoots together. There is also a new breed of production for CGI studios who are making it all within computer software 3D. Outside broadcast companies as well, so typically dealing with live events such as sports and ceremonies. There are a couple of different types of production companies to get involved with, especially if you like to be near the content and the talent. Maybe you want to simply start from the bottom and be a runner, a production assistant, or rigger, then this is the place to go have a look at any programme's end credits for pointers.

If you really want to work in broadcast media which type of company are you aiming for, can you picture yourself in a workplace that you'd be happy working in?

Ancast Insight

This could be a common theme throughout your career; it's likely you may work for more than one type of company, as many role types transcend companies and even industry. A lot of people have an obsession with aiming straight away for the biggest broadcaster or studio; the BBC has this affinity a lot with candidates. It's like people are having a bit of FOMO (or fear of missing out) or a sense of worth, getting a job with a big studio or public broadcaster, but as I will testify, other ways are more rewarding.

During both my university degrees, I found paid freelance work, mostly in live events, sometimes barely breaking even, but it meant I had clients who came back more and more. They offered other work through affiliates and mutual contacts and recommendations. So after leaving university, I got even more commercial clients and built up a brand and portfolio that spurred on much collaboration with industry and alumni colleagues. We were invoicing and subcontracting work to each other to satisfy our respective client briefs. We all had a specialist freelance sort of brand; between us, we had a production kit and some post-production gear. Also, some coders in the mix that we could all compliment each other's services with, basically bouncing work off each other.

Once I moved to London, the type of company that I worked for changed, so it switched to either being a broadcaster or a service provider consistently for over a decade now. For many years, I'd got my experience under my belt with service providers. More recently, over the past couple of years, I dealt with contractor or consultancy assignments with broadcasters like Discovery, ViaSat, and Channel Four. It reinforces that your skill moves with you from company to company because they're all broadcast industry companies at the end of the day, just different types.

I tend to find the service providers are at the beck and call of their clients but have diverse technology solutions and projects. That contrasts with broadcasters who bring scale, and they are well resourced with due diligence on the high-profile nature of their output, essentially. These are the typical types of broadcast companies that you could meander between throughout your career. Later, I'll cover how to best target those and get them in a search matrix, so you'll be able to figure out which ones you might have more luck with.

4. TYPES OF WORK

Types of work

I find this is grouped into three main levels of employment status, hours worked, and industry-specific. So do you want to be a full-time, permanent, paid employee, or do you want to be an independent consultant?

The Inside Track

An excerpt from Ancast's podcast with Melissa Carr giving her real-life insight.

Melissa Carr: "So how do you get into professional services in the media industry?"

Tip one: operational experience.

"I would say that if that is your end goal, get some operational experience in the media industry. It's not the route I followed, but if that's what you want to do, you need to learn about how different departments work. Get to understand a bit more about the culture of the different types of teams, get into the detail of work processes and try to look for any improvements that you can highlight to your managers and the people that you work with. If you've got the time, start to write up your suggestions. Not everything will be feasible, but at least it proves that you've got an enquiring mind and a focus on improving the working situation."

Tip two: volunteer to work on projects.

"If there's any kind of significant change happening in your business or departments, the chances are that subject matter experts, people who know the business, who understand the operations are going to be required to participate in those, by giving information or helping with testing or something similar. That's how I got involved - that was my Siemens experience. Once you start working with analysts or project managers or testers or developers, you'll start to understand more about the dynamics of projects. You'll start to get a bit more of a feel for the areas that you're most interested in."

Tip three: training.

"If you've got the opportunity and your manager's supportive, then ask for some training in business analysis or project management. You can pay for courses yourself as well, but there's lots of free training that's worth taking a look at."

'Broadcast Media: The Inside Track' Podcast published 5th April 2021 on various platforms

Payroll (PAYE/FTC) v Self Employed

You could be employed full or part-time on the payroll as Pay As You Earn (PAYE) or on a Fixed Term Contract (FTC). Both of these mean you're taxed at source, you don't have to worry about your tax, it's all done through HR, and you just get the net payment in the bank typically once a month. It's quite simply down to which tax code you are on when you see your payslips from payroll every time.

But for the self-employed, if you're a freelancer, sole trader, consultant, or contractor, then you do have to manage your own taxes, which comes with trade-offs. These are typically the employee benefits; if you're on the payroll, you get paid holiday, you'll have the pension, the sick pay, and then you may get some other incentives such as medical covers and a car, perhaps. But if you are in charge of your own taxes and you're self-employed, you do have control of what work you do and when, but you don't get paid time off. So as you don't get holiday pay, sick pay, pension, and things like that, you'll have to pay for other insurances and make sure you're contributing your own pension funds as well. So that's the misnomer that consultants, contractors, and freelancers are overpaid, but actually, they have all these other costs and trade-offs that they've got to compensate for in other ways. The biggest risk is job security, as these are short assignments, no guarantee of more work, and often the first to go if budget cuts are happening.

Static Hours (Office) v Antisocial

Another angle on types of work is between static hours (think office hours, Monday to Friday 9 'til 5) and anti-social hours—outside these hours. Office hours are obviously very steady, very predictable. You know where you are going every time you turn up, and by and large, that's what a lot of people in the industry are working to and indeed the general population. Versus antisocial hours, these job types could be 'on call' or they could be shift work. This could mean early, mid and late shifts through the day or night and either in the week or on the weekend. Particularly the production work with filming live events for TV which typically takes place on the weekend. So bear in mind that if you're constantly working on the weekend, you've got to compensate on the other days to preserve a work-life balance as well as other commitments that you might have.

Broadcast Niche v Industry Agnostic

Then there's another specifically broadcast type of work I've described as a niche as opposed to industry agnostic. Specific types definitely include the production side, as you can't lift and shift that to other industries; other examples could be a manufacturer's broadcast engineer or architecture roles. Think of the industry-agnostic types of work, like in HR for a broadcast company—that's going to be very similar to working for an HR company anywhere in any other company or industry. This applies to working in accounts, office admin, finance, facilities, security, and IT in general to an extent. It generally follows roles that transcend the industry essentially, so you could take your skills if you didn't like the broadcast industry and move on elsewhere. It's the same with people coming into the industry; if they have some IT skills in another type of industry, then their CV and their interview would be on their agnostic IT skills, which they could bring to the broadcast industry. It's worth noting if you're going after a very niche type of broadcast work, they're the most difficult to secure.

Other Paths

Some other paths to mention are collaborations where you partner with trusted associates and perhaps get a round of funding. There are all sorts of Arts Council and similar grants available that you might be able to split a couple of hundred or a couple of thousand pounds and produce something off the back of it together. It's another source of work and good to reflect on your CV with its entrepreneurship edge. You could build a brand or product if you've got a concept for an idea; it may be worth pursuing if you've got the business acumen to promote that and try to make it a viable product.

There are startups as well; I've been approached quite a few times to be a co-founder at a startup. Especially if they get good funding, then they will be hiring fairly quickly. So you'll need good judgment and also a commitment to progress quickly. But there are some very exciting startups around, and your promotions are likely to be faster if successful, note both these may need investor pitches which means your business skills must be finely tuned.

With all the above areas try to find their networking events; get the inside track, as it's a very dynamic area to work in. It is also possible for newcomers to train up and get new skills in for example cloud computing which transcends any industry but you could then carve out your niche in broadcast. Also, broadcast media agencies are in the industry as well; they are a very specialist area to get, but definitely worth it if you're a people person as well.

Have you thought of what the job roles structure and working pattern would be, why not assess your circumstances and make sure you find the most suitable one?

Ancast Insight

I was thinking of direct stories, but it's a great opportunity to show you how other people have approached this. To give you a good analogy consider: Sir Christopher Wren, who slipped in with the labourers building St Paul's and asked them what they were doing. One remarked, "Helping Sir Wren build a beautiful cathedral," and that's because that labourer had a vision, he knew he had a part to play, and he was happy. He asked some other labourers who simply said, "cutting stone" or "earning 10 shillings."

To try and draw parallels with those working styles, as I discovered with working antisocial hours, I found that it wasn't for me. After being PAYE most of my adult life, I had an opportunity to be my own boss and took it, but now I am responsible for my own taxes and accounting. I also knew I didn't want a standard skillset, and my personal brand was a niche by its nature. Finally, I did want to start working standard office hours in broadcast projects with no direct reports, and that's where I've found my happy place, and so can you.

5. COMPETENCY

Your Competency – Can You Do The Work?

The three 'C's' are the major pillars to making your moves in your career. The first C is Competency, 'can you do the work?' plain and simple. This is where you're best off carving out a niche, a bespoke competency and as highlighted before, it's your personal brand essentially.

The Inside Track

An excerpt from Ancast's podcast with Phil Hodgetts giving his real-life insight.

Phil Hodgetts: I think you've got to be open. If I was to go back to myself when I was kind of 17, 18, or even at University, I think I would be telling myself to not pin my hopes on one certain dream. I have a North star. That North star might be to, you know, have a mortgage, a house and a family by the age of 30 or something like that.

Or it might be to be a CEO of Sky or Discovery or whatever that North star might be, of course, [to] have something like that in mind, but understand that the journey is never just a linear thing to get you to that point. You know, you, there's ups, and there's downs all around, you know, you're on a roller coaster the whole way through.

And [to] follow my gut instinct and know that even if it feels like it's a risky decision that I make and I'm making the right decision at that moment, at that point in time. No one ever told me that back then, I was just kind of falling into one thing to the other.

And that's good experience equally as well, I never had a definite until I - this is going to sound really kind of silly - but until I knew that. I did want that four bedroom detached house with a driveway that was a decent walk to the beach and my family to grow up in a nice area. That was, that's been the only thing that I've really pinned on and gone - I'm going to continue, and I'm going to work for that. So, you know, you've just got to be open-minded when you're young, haven't you really?

'Broadcast Media: The Inside Track' Podcast published 22nd March 2021 on various platforms

Bespoke Competency

This is all about understanding your work style, personal values, and team roles, then actually playing to the strengths as well, so use it to your advantage. There are a number of different ways you can figure out what your personal values are and what your work style is. Like some of the Myers-Briggs type assessments online, you could look for building character profiles or even look at tools to find your strengths and what motivates you. These are all tools to figure out what's driving you underneath essentially. I've had some ways that I've found this out for myself, such as my personal work style, which was done from one of the courses that I attended years ago.

So, for example, typical team roles were described as plant or resource investigator, monitor, evaluator, coordinator, shaper, team worker, implementer, and specialist phrases. You can also combine a few of those as well, and you'll get your 2 nearest plant/resource investigator, for example. Personal values can come from similar tools. These can be integrity, education, diligence, focus, personability, etc. There was a strength development tool where you focus on relating a style and a rewarding environment. So it could be altruistic and nurturing, assertive and directing, analytic and autotomizing, flexible and cohering or cautious and supporting.

It gives you a motivational value system—almost like a compass and helps you prevent vulnerable moments as well. That's one of the key things: finding your strengths and understanding them, what motivates you, and how to deal with conflict. Write them down and think back on where you have overcome obstacles, taken action, and gotten results from them. You need to write down some concrete stories and specific examples of this. It could be from previous projects where something unexpected happened, and you thought about how to deal with it and took action that resulted in something positive.

It could be something in a previous job role or project, it could be something unrelated, but it should emphasize the fact that you think laterally. You see the big picture; you can logically deal with obstacles and find a way around it essentially. So it's good to write down a few of these, especially if you're linking it back to your CV, which again shows that you are competent in dealing with situations.

It's good to rehearse these as well, so get them written down, read it through, read it back to yourself. Long-term aspirations are another thing that's in the mix; hiring managers are keen to know what those long-term aspirations are.

It emphasizes that you're a driven person, and they also may help with giving confidence that you might like to stay in that particular role or company and not just going to be there for a short period of time. It's good to have five questions in your back pocket; these should be based on what your competency is. It's always good to have a couple of standard questions in your arsenal to ask anyone whom you're networking with, interviewing with, discussing socially, or even with old colleagues. It's always good to understand what you can gain and improve your competency with by using a couple of standard questions that you can just ask at any point, even to fill silences.

Leading on from nurturing your competency is researching other job titles. If you are not sure of the road to your ideal job role, then have a look at a few of the titles, have a look at your LinkedIn connections, or ask around your network and figure out how they got there. If you really want to be a systems architect or a producer or any sort of broadcast media profession, then looking at how people got there might give you an indication of how to tailor your competency, maybe gain some extra skills, or start to get some experience in other areas, in order to achieve your career goal.

Brainstorm places to work as well, as it's always good to have an idea of places where certain specialist skills or certain competencies are, some renowned places that might be sought after. Also, finding out through your network what it's like to work there as well. The key thing to nail is the question that comes up most often; 'Tell me about yourself.' All the broadcast and media hirers, will read your CV, and they'll probably read what you did last. They'll know your profile, and they'll know where you last worked, but this goes a little bit deeper than that. So, definitely rehearse the response to "tell me about yourself." It could sort of be tailored more towards the job that you're going for as well, the opportunity that you are interviewing for.

So, when they ask you that, you have rehearsed, "Well, I'm a..." even if you are not in a current position where you have this particular job title. Maybe you are between work, or maybe you're aspiring to get into that area, but you've got all the previous experience to have that role. Then when you explain "I am a.." it should be in the voice of that particular job title or job role.

Ancast Insight

My insight into this is having been an employee representative previously at a broadcast service provider. I was fortunate enough to be put forward for a leadership course, where one of their exercises was self-perception. Having filled it in, I got the report back at work after the course finished, and it was a true reflection of my personal style. It talked about exercising creative disposition, achieving professionalism, being at the forefront of new developments, and not being suited to admin or managerial roles. I was in front of my manager at the time, so I got him to read it, and I saw him kind of realizing that this totally described who I was. It really made me sit up and think, "Yeah, this is me."

It read: "Your profile shows that you gain great intrinsic satisfaction from the nature of the work in which you're engaged. For you, work is like a hobby, offering you a chance to exercise your creative disposition and to achieve professionalism all at the same time. For as far as the outside world is concerned, you will be known and respected for your knowledge of the special skills and the fact that you are at the forefront of most new developments. The limitations you may have to accept apply to your administrative and managerial skills. The greater the burdens placed upon you outside your area of professional and technical competence, the greater the likelihood that you will encounter criticism, whether overt or implied.

This means you may have to make a conscious choice in terms of the direction of your career. A wider arena would offer broader prospects of advancement, but you would also face stiffer competition, and you may well lose some of your professional expertise. The alternative is to build up your own personal reputation in your own special area and carve out your own job within it. For the future, your best career path could well be as a consultant working either internally or externally; this will only be feasible if you can secure the respect of those who work in adjacent territories. They will need to know, in general terms, how you are progressing and what you have to offer. If you are to make your mark, bear in mind that one lesson which others like you apt to forget; never blind people with science or flood them with technical details that carry no real interest. Knowing where to draw the line is a real art.

Your operating style is that of a pioneering professional. Colleagues will respect you for what you know and what you have achieved. But beyond that circle, you may find difficulty in reaching out to others. Yet, there is a way of doing this. The secret lies in communicating in a way people outside your area of expertise can understand, make a point of presenting a concise overview when clarity of message is required. On a final note, you need to take account of the role for which you are least suited. You do not appear to have the characteristics of a hard-driving executive who obtains insults by power and pressure. If you can work in harmony with somebody who has these compliment qualities, your own performance is likely to improve."

Another telling report was detailing my strengths on the character profile: "has innovative tendencies and needs to work in a mentally challenging environment" and "Performs best on his own, or when in a team given the freedom to exercise his particular skill," also, "Suited to work where he can use his acquired knowledge to follow a professional career path." It was an eye-opener reading the possible weakness: "uncomfortable when having to deal with pressure" and "check-in interview, show interest in the specific areas of Ben Anchor's previous work then switch to probing about eventual outcomes." So what happens in the end? Well, the report advised me to try to find out whether efforts and study led to anything notable or even whether there was a worthwhile outcome in mind, in which case say, "tell me about the main obstacles."

Finally, the character profile details on placement were; "should be treated as a clever expert and placed in a position where that expertise can be used to advantage. If the appointment requires more general qualities, a key factor likely to affect the performance of a Ben Anchor will be the character of his intended work associate. In the event of a close working relationship, the compatibility factor will override more technical considerations." It also noted "checking the two people are happy with the association and the terms of reference before the appointment is finalized."

I've also been described as a plant specialist where a 'Plant' is creative, imaginative, unorthodox, solves difficult problems, a specialist is single-minded, self-starting, and dedicated. That's my team role profile, and this really helped me on my way, it made me understand what drives me underneath, and that's how I managed to make some major moves since then.

Portfolio

When we think of a portfolio, we often think of our school and university folders, papers, drawings, artwork, and photography, but in the industry, we all have to present our broadcast media work to the hirers every so often. It leads back to the questions they will have—what skills do you possess, what have you done lately, and is it relevant here? There are many ways this can be exhibited to the hirer, whether that's a conversation, viewing of work in an online portal or by reading a document that you've authored yourself.

Some of your work may only be relevant to 1 or 2 'outlets' to show potential managers that "yes I can do the work"—and here it is and it can easily be revealed. It must be readily accessible, easily listened/watched, or made easy to read, as the attention time you get is short, and you must make it count; otherwise, they'll get turned off or move onto the next. In any case, you should have your portfolio easily describable in conversation so if you're caught by surprise, always have that piece of work you can easily and with confidence talk about.

This is where you can build up your own web presence on talent portals, YouTube, your own website, and your own stationery, perhaps as well. I've tended to get some business cards even when I was a sole trader, and in the early days, it projects a professional image. Then over time, over the years, I've developed more and more professional-looking websites, listed profiles with all the relevant services. Got quality portfolios and client work on there that you could also create with little web authoring knowledge using template style websites such as Wix and Squarespace.

With many different disciplines in broadcast media, you'll need to find the right one for your portfolio; it will differ if you're a creative making content than say technical, operational, or office-based roles. Obvious video platforms include Vimeo, Daily Motion, and YouTube, and for audio, think of podcast platforms, Soundcloud, Bandcamp, and Mixcloud—all embeddable, making it a good playback experience. There are several 'talent' style sites where you can register, such as Media Match, Production Hub, Mandy, Staff Me Up, Crewing Company, Grapevine, as well as newcomers like Hired and Juno.

For the roles whose output is not so much audio or visual, then your focus could be more text and image-based methods. It could be articles that you have written to demonstrate how you delivered a technical, operational, or editorial piece of work that can be accessible by a URL and have the right imagery and narrative to it. There are many social media groups too that you can post in as well as industry publications and trade show material that you could use as an outlet for your work.

Your LinkedIn profile speaks volumes as well; a very basic LinkedIn with no picture and none of the extras that LinkedIn provides looks like there's been no effort put in there. People search through LinkedIn and often, so they're actually by default looking at your profile there as well.

Your CV may also have a portfolio and need a professional email as well, so do away with those childhood email addresses that don't look too great. Once you order domains, they don't cost too much these days, they can be plugged into the Gmail backend, so it's a very well-functioning email system.

Think deep down what your competency is and what your core skills are, this is displayed by your personal brand so ask yourself what are my strongest talents?

Ancast Insight

I have some direct insight into my portfolio to show you how it worked getting it out there. My first business card had a strapline on it: "The Broadcast Change Agent," as it was my personal style of Technology—Projects—Specialist. When I had a moment to project a better professional image, I cleaned up my social channels, updated my email to the domain name, formatted the signatures to HTML, and put in all the 'don't print' and legal jargon at the bottom as well. Then I also launched my own website, which took a few days but at least gave me a web presence. I knew I was also gaining some new skills by making a website that was desktop, tablet, and mobile compatible; it was fully secure, had contact pages on it, and was quite functional actually.

Even if you have your own domain in an email address, any connections are likely to perhaps try the web address of your email as well, just to have a look. I use Squarespace, which by default had Squarespace in the URL, but you're able to also configure your own domains there. There are other ones out there like Wix, or you can possibly go to the freelance market as well.

Without actually promoting my website to industry colleagues, some of them just turned around and said, "How did you create that? It looks really good." I just explain that I did it myself, and you know these template websites. As they know what they're doing, they take care of all that complexity in the background, but you've got to spend some time on the front end, making it look good. People notice these things, and so you never know who that person might be—it might be the call out of the blue that everybody waits for.

Your Broadcast Media CV

Curriculum Vitae Style

First of all, you will never really finish your CV/résumé, as it will change over time as you gain and move between broadcast roles. Besides, you will come up with different iterations as you come up with different ways to present it. Your CV could fall into a functional style, a chronological style, or a mix of both—if you're fresh from a course or switching industry, you may have more luck with a functional style. Hirers typically filter out the vast amount of candidates by looking at CVs, so they spend about 7 seconds on reading it and up to 30 seconds if it caught their attention, mostly from your profile and on the last place you worked. So this is where you really need to make sure it stands out and make a lot of effort to solve their hiring needs.

For the makeup of the CV itself, then there are a few gotchas that are easily missed or need to be excluded. To make that brief viewing time count, then:

- Be careful about aesthetics. Avoid photos on your profile unless you are talent. Also, no funny fonts, unnecessary colours, or graphics—some subtle design may be permissible if you're a creative.

- Have white space. It's good to have some in there, so don't make it a big block of text all the way through multiple pages; make it concise and actually give some space within it to breathe.

- Create a good clear header. This will include contact details such as your name, mobile phone number, and a professional email address (make a new free one if you have a jokey/inappropriate or only have an academic one).

- Concentrate on examples. These are where you've solved something, saved time and money for any previous projects, productions, or even casual jobs you've had previously, where you can detail any soft skills you developed.

- Highlight recent experience. This can be unpaid or paid, but don't simply list the duties, instead, spell out how you went above and beyond and list them out using bullet points, adding what you brought extra to that role

- List recent relevant qualifications. So if it's university, no need to list GCSEs, etc., also professional certifications make you stand out too. If you don't have any, then have a couple of testimonials quoted; this might also back you up and give you the edge.

A typical broadcast media hirer is looking at the position they need to fill to see if you've had experience and skills listed in your CV to match. That's why it's always good to tweak your profile slightly to the role, to make things stand out and flag the attention of the hiring manager. It applies to a cover letter, where you can give the hirer some context and gives you another opportunity to explain why your skills relate to the function the role is trying to fill, and why you are a good fit.

Ancast Insight

It took me so many versions of my CV to get it to an optimal place, so here's some of my insight. It's probably dozens and dozens of times before you get to a form of your CV that is getting results, which means you are getting at least phone interviews or first interviews, and it's sort of finessing this over time.

Your CV is about conveying your competency, and it includes all the talking points that hiring managers are looking for. For me it was about a lot of feedback and learning what triggers the interview request. Some of the feedback has come from recruiters, some of the feedback has come from after interviews, some of the feedback has come from your network essentially. I found that making your profile really about your personal style helps focus the hirer. Explaining on a literal level why you can fill this position based on writing it in a matter-of-fact way that is concise and punchy.

I started including tailored business skills and technical skills with bullets that then give the hiring manager an immediate bulleted list of the headlines of these particular skills. These are listed under my profile as 'Technical Skills' and 'Business Skills' and helped define the sort of work I was going for, in my case, the conduit between people and technology. It really focused the mind of the hiring manager, and I've kept that in until this day, and it has become a winning formula.

The next main area of focus is job history, this is the section you home in on, bringing recent experience to the role they want to fill, and you've got to write what they want to hear. So obviously, don't make up anything, as that will most likely come back on you, but they are going to market to find a person to fill this particular job role. If you can tailor your job history with solutions they need, then write it as such and include those things that you can link with their job description. It could be where you've come up with a different or novel approach, mention of relevant technology, or anything that would kind of relate to the job post essentially.

Your LinkedIn Makeover

LinkedIn Style

Your LinkedIn is separate from your CV; it's a more personal and conversational style more than anything. CVs are written in the third person tense; your LinkedIn should be more in the first-person perspective. Writing it from the heart in many ways, it's about what makes you tick, and the more informal setting will also help build your network and find more out than just what's on your CV.

Acquaintances then reach out to new ones. For example, when following people and companies and interacting, you'll then get people looking at your LinkedIn profile. This then will convey your personal brand with LinkedIn bringing your profile to life with the right privacy settings, whereas your standard 2-page CV can be a bit dry.

There are practical aspects of making LinkedIn work for you by setting it up in the best possible way, these include:

- Be accessible. This is to make sure your profile is public and discoverable; try Google your name or look in incognito mode. Add as many contact details as possible and use a custom URL that is short and sweet.

- Make it look appealing. First off, definitely add a professional photo and use the % filled-in feature to complete your profile. If you're in broadcast media, use the multimedia functions but ensure it's not too overbearing.

- Make a good header. As with your CV, most people will only read the first section of it, so get a catchy headline and put a lot of thought into the summary, which could hook them in.

- List work achievements. Go beyond job duties and spell out your accomplishments with bullet points on what you did and how you did it. Link people who you worked for or with as hirers can often pick this up too.

- Use the additional features; there is space to list out languages, volunteering, projects, and qualifications. Also, use the recommendation function so people can give you a glowing reference; try to get a mutual trusted contact to write yours.

- Go and network, try and get as many people you actually know to connect, as seeing only 10's of connections is not very appealing. Also, join groups, post content, comment, and join conversations that will help grow your network.

The more you engage with the LinkedIn community, the better your network grows, connections turn into conversations, and who knows where they'll lead. The LinkedIn platform's algorithms are good at making it work for you the more you use it. The instant messenger function is another great feature, and within a few message exchanges, sometimes your luck can change, especially if your profile radiates 'open to work.'

Ancast Insight

Thinking of my insights in my career development, it's been fascinating since I started using it in 2006 after leaving university in 2004. We can draw parallels with the advent of social media; the professional version of that is here on LinkedIn, what was a static website, has now become a professional networking platform.

From the early days, I just created a profile on it, and that was the extent of it, as I didn't appreciate its value back then. The features now and the algorithms that it's got are improving and making it much easier for everyone to connect and make full use of the tools on the platform. So when I have downtime or feel I need to maintain my page, I'll update the profile and the recent job history; this activity update then ripples out on the feed to my network. A simple technique is updating your LinkedIn headline to 'Available' or similar as it advertises this when messaging and interacting with people on the platform. Having messaged an old manager who noticed it we then met the next day, I was invited down and was having coffee with a broadcast consultancy firm needing new consultant associates.

This was just on the back of seeing that I was 'Available' and plugging a gap they needed; after a quick chat on LinkedIn, it facilitated a meeting—I didn't have their regular contact details, so the interaction was only possible this way. Having these chance interactions then instigated more leads, which led to more possible job openings and a chance of networking. I've made posts on LinkedIn, and old colleagues have texted me about it, so here's me thinking nobody reads them, but people do. I had one instance where a broadcast TX operation I previously worked in closed, so I posted a photo of my old shift colleagues that I worked with on it. It triggered more interactions, profile views, comments, and likes. On a basic networking level, it was just maintenance and a chance to reconnect with some old colleagues. Coincidentally, I was talking about it on a contractor assignment at the time, and another contractor had seen that I put the picture up as well! So LinkedIn is good to learn early on, as it really stands out; it's a very powerful tool and has its own style to it.

6. COMPATIBILITY

Your Compatibility – Can You Do The Work Here?

The conversation has now moved on, your CV gets you in the door, it has demonstrated to the broadcast media hirer that you 'can you do the work' and they have sifted through CVs and got a short list for an interview. If you've overcome that hurdle, then your next C is for Compatibility, 'can you do the work here?'

This is where you need to do your research, and one of the first things that provide the most useful insights is your industry sources. These can be where you can sign up for subscriptions, online news, free publications, newsletters, webinars, and maybe even some print publications.

The Inside Track

An excerpt from Ancast's podcast with Michael Kosmides giving his real-life insight.

Michael Kosmides: My colleagues, the other lecturers as well are either journalists that moved into academia, like myself or journalists who are still working.

And that's very important. Just imagine the media industry remembering how it was, let's say, 20 years ago. It's a completely different environment and experience I had in that environment. It's still valuable, but it's a bit more historic than current for a student to really get something good for them.

For something to be valuable to them in terms of getting a new job, you need to be current all the time, and you need to bring that experience and make it current. I obviously give loads of examples from my own experience, and I invite other journalists to come every now and then and speak about their own experiences about their own stuff.

And that works because it's a great actually living experience for the student and provides good information. In fact, the feedback we've got from the students is that these are the things they really want to learn. We try to incorporate it in the course, with support from a lot of local newspapers and local media, because as we know, they are really under threat, especially in the current circumstances.

We've had, for example, the editor of the South London News join us and do a master class bringing his own experience about what he does every day, which was so incredibly valuable for the students - they really loved it. We give them the opportunity of getting placements and writing articles with their own by-lines from year one in local posts, like Southwark News, which again is one of our other local media (local, I mean to the University, to London South Bank University). It's very important to bring this current sense of the job to students.

For me, and this is something that I tell them from day one, "you don't have to consider yourself a student, you have to consider yourself a journalist". And that's the only way forward for me. A young person joining the university or just starting in the industry is a journalist. Simple as that. Maybe with not as much experience or knowledge, fair enough. That will come. But if you start thinking as a journalist, then everything will start making sense.

And then, at the end of the day, coming back to the example of University and studies, you will not bother so much about what grade you're going to get. You will bother about getting a good story. If it's well written, news worthy, it will get a good grade. You don't have to bother about ticking boxes or what exactly they are asking. It doesn't matter. All we are asking as a journalist is to get a good story that is relevant to the audience, the viewers, the readers, whatever it is that you've got.

'Broadcast Media: The Inside Track' Podcast published 1st March 2021 on various platforms

Industry Sources

Especially during the pandemic, there are a lot more webinars available these days; most of them are free to attend. They are useful because of who the speakers are. They may work in your target companies, companies you want to work for, and it's where you may get some insights or get the inside track. It's also useful looking at the guest list as well; there might be some people in the participants' list that you could become acquainted with.

Also, in-person events such as trade shows are invaluable; some of the most famous ones are IBC in Amsterdam every September and the big North American one, NAB in April. Then there are other ones like Cannes Film Festival, Media Production Show, MIPCOM, CABSAT and numerous other ones around the world. This is where I attend in-person demos, and this is where the most unexpected networking takes place. Just meeting brand-new connections off chance encounters that get conversations started about job leads or work contracts.

Some other events are listed sometimes on listings sites like Eventbrite, and you can also check out meetup.com for one-off or series meetings. There are a few broadcast media and technology networking events happening on a local level, such as Soho Media Club in London. There are some new offerings from IABM for the trade association events but also LinkedIn Live, which offers a live broadcast facility on the platform.

Then the other source industry sources are your own contacts in your own network. It may be useful to keep in conversation with the recruitment agencies; they might give you some insight into what might be in the pipeline. What clients are asking the recruiters for and also friends that are currently employed as well. It's useful to have colleagues or industry connections that you may speak to help give you some insight into industry news, essentially what's happening in their company or in their domain.

Target Matrix

What's next is to do a target matrix of these companies, so you need to define and focus on targeting a top 10 list or top 20 or 30 list. Create an expandable matrix of contacts and companies; this is so you've always got something to work on. Typical things in a target matrix might include the company name, the location, the company's size, the type of company, and details of first, second, and third-line contacts. One being the most valuable, possibly hiring managers, the second being people you may know there, and the third contacts might be just trying to reach out to new people in those companies. Once you have a good understanding of the type of company you want to work for, then you can start to understand if there are any resource demands coming from your network and from your industry sources. That might actually make you bump up the priority, so you need to make some connections there. You can typically do it in Excel or an online spreadsheet like Google docs.

I built up a broadcast companies matrix, and then I also had another tab with the same type of details on it, but for recruitment agencies for managing the context and the low down of what's happening with the different recruitment agencies. Then the third tab I actually had was a post-production house; this was an option if I wanted to go back to that sort of work. If I wasn't getting very many leads on the broadcast side, then at least I could start building out a network there and expanding the matrix based on previous skills that I had. So it's possible you can have multiple tabs to maintain these different contacts across those companies, which gives you more avenues to pursue and crucially options.

Grow Your Network

The next thing that comes off the back of that is growing your network. It's a good idea to reach out to a number of different contacts per week. Ideally, to meet in person (as people like the personal side), but online is fine for convenience or in a global pandemic. So, if you are getting on with someone who you're networking with and there's some good rapport, and you feel like you can add them on LinkedIn, just maybe add them straight away—everyone's got a smartphone these days. Otherwise, a contact might go stale; if you leave it a few days or a week or two to follow up by an email, it's likely to get ignored. So strike while the iron is hot; if these people have got interesting and overlapping things in common with what you're discussing, then just add them there and then.

The other ways are to follow articles as well; it could be some discussion on a thread, for example. You could actually make a genuine connection based on conversations on comments and threads. You can ask, "Can we Link In?" and they'll probably say yes, and you can get instant messaging straight away.

The aim is to make your way through this matrix, start filling it up, and maintaining which day you contacted who, what was the outcome, plus any review dates. Add some notes, possibly around resourcing and if there are any opportunities there because otherwise, you may just prioritize one over the other.

There could be some huge companies in there with many openings and many contacts, which may need more time to maintain in your target matrix. But certainly making contact by platform messaging, phone, and email depending on how suitable each one is. They'll be contacts and possibly a good deal more for actually making connections on LinkedIn or other professional platforms which you will then see on your news feed.

Gain Knowledge

As well as growing your network, this is gaining knowledge, as knowledge is power, and you need to be on top of the industry game essentially. If you've got the real inside information, then you will have the edge that could be crucial in an interview. So keep on track of new developments, mergers and acquisitions, new technology, company announcements, and product launches. This all gives you the inside track, which is always noticed by broadcast hirers who are normally ahead with industry developments, and if you have the inside info, it turns heads.

The more knowledge you soak up like a sponge, the more it will stick in your mind, and there's a chance that you might be asked for it in an interview or when you're talking to someone in your network or at an event. If you know the answer and you've got the knowledge, then there'll be some degree of respect and appreciation that you're on top of the game. Always sign up to any of those places where you can get this knowledge from, again looking at the industry sources.

Get Yourself Out There

Start mixing in your network with something as simple as sharing knowledge and get yourself out there. This is free after all; reposting and sharing useful articles etc., doesn't cost anything. In fact, it might even spark off some conversations in itself. Remember the 'I am a..' mantra, so even though you're looking for work, don't forget that you are actually who you say you are, and this is your passion, and this is who you are. So it's like you're not jobless; it's about how you've got to approach it. So if you want to be that producer or an engineer or a developer, whatever it is, even if, for example, you're getting some small producer gigs somewhere, then that's who you are. 'I'm a producer…' So try to think in that mindset when you are getting yourself out there, and you're explaining who you are, that all stems from your competency.

Research and fill in the blanks with your contacts, as this is looking for connections that might get you in front of a hiring manager. If you make a connection and they've got something good to demonstrate, then you might ask for a demonstration, see if you want to go down to the office. Ask subtly for some contacts around your target company, follow up on LinkedIn. Some people like WhatsApp and find it a lot more personable, so don't be afraid to put yourself out there like that.

You have your sales pitch now like new friends you need to go and find people and companies who you like working with - but how will you find those matches?

Ancast Insight

There are many insights to give, but they all link back to knowing your competency; it makes mapping out the ideal place to work easier to whittle down. Having that spreadsheet and reaching out to old and new contacts in those companies works, having used this method it really works.

So prior to securing a new consultancy opportunity, I did exactly this and had around 20 on my list and around five recruiters. I had three levels of contacts, primary, secondary, and tertiary, to indicate how close to a hiring manager or updates the recruiters were giving. Then through publicly available information, by looking through press releases, events they hosted, and what mutual contacts advised me, it gave me a picture of where I should focus my attention.

In any given week, I was messaging brand new contacts on LinkedIn about developments or working practices for broadcast manufacturers and their products. I was also messaging connections about sports broadcast media events, even direct email and calling sales and managing directors at service providers.

This resulted in being invited to lunch and opening up discussions on where I can fit into a project in LA; this is straight off the back of building this matrix up. Perhaps old colleagues, course mates or just friends can give you an introduction, by any means, to hiring managers in broadcast media companies. It can then open up getting an idea of what the company is like, and if you will like working there too.

7. CHEMISTRY

Your Chemistry – Can You Do The Work Here With Us?

This is where your personality, team roles, and your character profile come through. Your CV only gets you in the door, really, and the chemistry in the interview is everything.

Interpersonal Soft Skills

You may have heard people talk about soft skills; these are also called interpersonal, transferable, non-cognitive, people, or essential skills, which are different from hard skills, also known as technical or competency-based skills. Hirers want to see these so they can make sure the candidate successful and good with customers and can work with the team. They include personality traits, personal attributes, and how well they communicate, which for the most part sums up how a person interacts with others. The obvious one is communication by listening, writing, presenting, and speaking clearly and politely—but non-verbal communication is also important. A good one is critical thinking that includes analysis, resourcefulness, problem-solving, adaptability, and in general, creativity. A main one is work ethic, so attentiveness, meeting deadlines, planning, punctuality, reliability, and general self-organizing. Another obvious one being teamwork, so awareness, social skills, collaboration, and dealing with difficulties. Some or all of the above may apply, but one thing everyone can have is a positive attitude that is as simple as courtesy, friendliness, respect, humour, patience, enthusiasm, and confidence.

So although hard skills are learned, these soft skills need developing, and although harder to learn, they are just as hard to measure or evaluate. Having said that, you can learn some of these skills by any other experience with people you may have, whether that's volunteering in your broadcast media field or from your academic groups. If your a newcomer but worked in public facing roles like hospitality, retail, transport, service sector then you have proven experience and you must list these on your CV so potential hirers can see that.

It's important to understand what makes you tick; this applies to any industry, but with so many characters in broadcast media, it's worth knowing how you fit in and playing it to your advantage. There is a domain-level personality type in 5 categories of openness, conscientiousness, extraversion, agreeableness, and neuroticism—you can find online tests for this to give you an indication. This gave me, for example, in the same order being traditional, careful/diligent, social/outgoing, friendly/optimistic, and emotional stability —all fairly accurate.

Delving a bit deeper, I found out I am a 'Protagonist' or an 'ENFJ-A' as the 16 personality types go; it was pretty accurate and only took me around 10 minutes to answer the online test questions. If you have wondered where those 4 letter codes come from, as some people put them on profiles, it's one of the 16 combinations of personality types detailed by the Myers-Briggs method.

It says my typical traits are leading, full of passion, natural confidence, guiding others to work together, inspiring others to achieve—typical of coaches and teachers. I am pleased to say that Barack Obama and The Oracle from the Matrix movie are also the same personality types! But for all the good things, my results also showed weaknesses such as performing poorly in pressurized situations and decision making as well as being too selfless. It really helps you reflect on your limits and focus on your strengths, which will prove invaluable in an industry that has some big personalities.

Once you get a better understanding of your values, character styles, and behaviours, it will better inform you on how you fit into team roles. These are generally in 3 groups of action-oriented roles (creating and maintaining teams), social orientated roles (supporting team performance), and thinking orientated roles (focused on task content). It's worth recognising that teamwork is about synergy and synchronizing energy, and when you join a team or group, that development together often follows Bruce Tuckman's theory of forming, storming, norming, performing, and adjourning.

Leading on from these is what motivates you; this question will often come up in interviews, so it's wise to understand it, as they will gauge what you value, enjoy doing, whether you'd do well in the role or the team. It's good to find out strengths around people, tasks, and processes but also competency-based motivations to have in your answers. On a basic level, it's why we do things, and these are linked to extrinsic and intrinsic rewards, with the latter better for performing meaningful work.

Whilst dealing with others, this may also throw up barriers, jarring difficult situations or times where it will show your weakness. Well, to counter this, knowing what you're less strong in will help you answer this in interviews and also deal with it in the often tense times of the industry. Perhaps ask yourself the things you avoid, what drains you or need help on, maybe do an online test to find out or ask an impartial acquaintance for their honest opinion and to identify it. If you lack competencies, you can learn some; if it's soft skills, you can overcompensate by increased organisation in meetings, for example. Keep at it, as the more you do it, the more comfortable you'll be, and finally, identify people to lean on and help you in sticky times.

One last area that is worth mentioning is being assertive, many who struggle with confidence and soft skills will find this the hardest. But it's a great way to create a win-win situation, as it puts your needs and other's needs in the frame; if it's one or the other, you end up with either aggressive or passive traits, respectively. A strong belief in your value to the team and your own self-confidence but finding the fine line between accepting your needs are not more important than others. When you can articulate the exact need, then raise it and set achievable goals and putting this forward politely and professionally, you will be more likely to succeed. Remember you can't control other's behaviour, so if your want or need triggers something off, don't rise to it and keep it cordial.

At the end of the day, the value comes from you; people have their own opinions. So here we need to do questioning and apply this to negotiate the job role, so it comes out with that win-win situation. It's all about the interview really and how you perform on the day, so make the two Cs the most important and prepare for it accordingly.

Interview Research

The preparation for the interview is key; you need to know the company inside out. Look at the background, the history, look at what they do and check out the people working there. I've been questioned in interviews about what I know about the company, and fortunately, I'd researched! It could be a basic read of the 'About' section of the website or something that is in the news recently that will demonstrate that you are actively searching and knowledgeable about the company. You'll probably need to tailor some of your examples that you'll have for that company. So look at the situations, tasks, actions and results you have dealt with in the past that closely aligns with the job role and description. With those lists of stories that you have got in your back catalogue, you can refine and practice them. Also, you'll probably need to rehearse the question 'why did you apply for the job?' this where you need to apply your benefits and link them to the solution that they need. Rehearsing the 'Who am I?', it's all about your profile and tailoring what you did last to this job opening.

It's the same for preparation online as for face to face and phone interviews, as you're likely to face the same line of questioning. One difference with Skype/Zoom/Teams etc. (any online video calls) is to prepare what's in shot so clean background, good headshot and clear audio. You must research for a second interview, too, although this likely be a more deep dive, and any guidance on preparation, e.g. presentations from the hirer or recruiter, would be advantageous. All these involve interaction with the hiring managers, though; it's all to do with chemistry. Whether it's applying for full-time work or applying as a contractor, freelancer or consultant, it follows the same fundamentals. I have been treating the way I approach interviews in the same way, so I use the same techniques as a contractor and consultant as I've done for full-time jobs previously.

Make sure you have questions ready for them as they tend to ask these at the end, and you should make sure you've got questions relevant to either the job you're applying for, things that you need some clarification on or possibly the things about the company in general. Not having any questions at the end would probably raise a flag, and there will probably be other candidates out there who have already got their questions lined up.

Interview Day Checklist

When it comes to the day of the interview pay attention to the non-verbal communication, you can have a bit of a pre-flight checklist to go through. Make sure you're well presented; I tend to do interviews dressed how I'd normally go into that workplace. So nowadays I wouldn't be wearing a suit and tie and typically be a collared polo or a shirt and blazer, black jeans and casual shoes. At first, I'd wear suits, but now as I'm more confident interviewing, I'm more comfortable in the clothes that I'd wear doing the actual job. Just before you go in, it's quite important to do a quick mirror check, as you don't want to be sat through an interview with your hair at an angle or some mark on your face or something like that. If you're going somewhere, then perhaps find a local coffee shop, or if you're quite early for the interview, you could maybe ask to use the bathroom.

Make sure your posture is good, no slouching obviously, and make sure you're seated in the right position, no yawning, that sort of thing. When you and the panel meet for the first time in reception or in the first minute of an online interview, some small talk is always good to avoid silence. Confirmatory eye contact is good throughout the interview; this also applies to virtual interviews as well but do it naturally.

The interview itself is an interactive discussion; it's not a Q & A from the hiring manager. It gives you a chance to engage and open up the conversation a little bit because this is where you build up a rapport. This might elicit some information from the hiring manager that wasn't in the job description, and you didn't know in the first place. So it could actually tease out some information, not only about the job but about the company and about the potential workplace that you could be working in—so it is a two-way conversation.

Bring across your enthusiasm; if there's a lighthearted moment, then great, just kind of roll with it. If they mention certain things about how broadcast companies and departments operate or talk about ways of working, try to follow up in the conversation and reinforce the message that you are also very keen and interested in this area. When you get asked something, it's very important to think and pause before giving your answer, don't start to answer straight away. You'll probably find you'll become a bit unstuck, so formulate your answer by pausing, and then your answer will be much better.

There's always some sort of difficult question that they will ask you. So, it'd be useful to turn your vulnerable question into a positive. One classic thing they may ask is, "What is your weakness?" And you should have prepared for this prior. I could say I'm too self-critical when it comes to doing my business analyst work, I could say I work early or work late, or I'm very rigid in my work ethic or something like that. It's always useful to have a weakness, but then show it as a benefit almost to the role or the company.

Closing the Interview

The allotted time comes quickly, and the hiring manager will want to wrap up and close the interview. If they are interested, this is where the discussion would normally move on to Compensation questions, the fourth 'C.' You'll need to be adept at handling negotiation about this because they'll ask you what salary you will be expecting, and you should have done your research.

Make sure you understand the typical ranges beforehand. There are some companies that work on pay grades, like the BBC, and some other places probably have a pay grading system. You can also find out from your network, recruiters, and your contacts roughly what sorts of salaries are being earned. Also, look at the job posting itself, was it listed with a range? If not, and it comes down to it, ask them for their range before giving yours. It's much better to understand what their budget is rather than you shooting from the hip and coming up with a generous salary where other candidates of similar caliber would have quoted within budget. If they're not willing to give their range, then you should give your range. By giving the hirer options, you indicate that you'd be looking for a salary range between so many thousands.

This would give you the possibility of being a frontrunner if it came down to a shortlist because the interviewer could well have a top 2 list, and if you have a range and the other has a fixed amount, it could swing it. They may want to shortlist you to go to a second interview, or they may want to make a decision based on the first. If that is the case and they weren't willing to share the salary, then you can leave it with a range you'd be happy with, and for them to decide that they might be able to make the offer to satisfy both parties.

At this point, it may be worth just asking about the other benefits that may offset this. So if they offer a very generous pension, a very good medical package, a car, options of stock, bonuses, then this might also help inform you of what salary range you could be asking for or narrow it down.

The final thing would be to re-emphasize as soon as you are leaving the interview that you would like the job. Saying it often leaves a good impression that you'd be very interested in getting the job and you'd be looking forward to hearing from them soon. It's to exude enthusiasm and leave a lasting impression as you exit the door, only then moving on to the next interview, keeping your options open.

You must factor in soft skills to get the job, you may have a strong portfolio or CV but to be 1st choice ask how you can improve and practice my interpersonal skills?

Ancast Insight

It is true that with practice, interviewing gets easier, as I have found over the years. But for me, the key is always preparation, so if it's one of your target companies, you should have a lot to talk about being genuinely interested in working there specifically. The standard openings of what you know about the company you're interviewing for, the 'tell me about yourself' sort of opening narrative, and what made you apply for the job role is universal, and that applies to every single interview I've been to and needs no introduction. What I've learned is being comfortable in the reality that you're about to sit down with some potentially great colleagues.

As the years have gone by, I don't wear the suits anymore, I go in clothes that I feel comfortable in, making me more relaxed. I've known other friends in different industries, entrepreneur types who actually turned up with his dog! But there you go, he stood out and with great personal skills (but no suit), then turning up being relaxed (and different) ended up landing some quite large contracts and projects. Not that the dog is going to be appropriate for you, but just trying to emphasize that being comfortable in the interview is really important.

Build rapport with the interview panel because you'll probably be working with them directly, day in day out, if it goes well. As I do in the lift on the way up, you can have a bit of chitchat about something unrelated. Some current events that might be happening, industry news, that sort of thing. Just get some conversation going that's not necessarily sat around the interview desk. I bring all these soft skills into that conversational style interview.

An example is when I got pulled up on an expired Cisco qualification, as I'd still listed my CCNA networking qualification on my CV. But there was an expiry date. It must have been around four years or something, but actually, I said there's a story attached to that. Having told the story, it made them laugh, and although not successful at that time, I have since gotten some other work. The main interviewer on the panel remembered me when I reached out to him after a follow-up LinkedIn connection I made with him after the unsuccessful interview years earlier. I told him what I was going through at the time, and he said he had no idea I was going through a redundancy when he interviewed me. Who knows if it may have been different but look how it turned out later, as I messaged a few years after, and he managed to get me some lecturing work at Ravensbourne University.

Another time, I prepared and had read an article on an updated specification that was a renowned broadcast industry-wide one. In the interview, I was challenged on it, but I corrected the interviewer this time. Not only was it about a file delivery method and the file format specification, but also, I was actually referring to the delivery speed. I knew I was right, and I demonstrated I was ahead of the industry developments and news. I was bringing them some new information, I was assertive, and it can be quite challenging in the interview saying, 'no, that's not the case,' but I said actually according to the news I read then, this was referring to the speed rather than the file format. Either the penny dropped, or with my steadfastness, we moved on in the interview. It sort of bred mutual respect, and we've connected on LinkedIn since and appreciates I did a good interview, although I didn't get the job at the time.

One last thing I like to do is at the end of the interview, if I feel like it's the place for me, I'll tell them straight away and say eye-to-eye, "I'm definitely interested in the job." Showing that you'd like to work there shows how keen your interest is in the role, it's like a confirmation thing just before I leave.

Don't be disheartened by the number of interviews that you may not succeed in because things in the interviews might also spark off some other conversations or referrals, or you may actually meet them another time. It may be a talking point, for example, and that's how you build up rapport and your network of broadcast media contacts. This is where you practice the Chemistry, and that's one of the most important 'C's in the interview process.

8. CONTINUATION

Keep Calm and Carry On

As described in the previous section, the key to giving a good interview is to review afterwards and to think above and beyond CVs when embarking on your search, research your next ones, and repeat the process.

The Inside Track

An excerpt from Ancast's podcast with Natasha Monaghan giving her real-life insight.

Natasha Monaghan: It's good to nurture people as they're going through a course or even at the point before they've decided what they're going to do. But they don't often come to me, you know before they already know what they're going to do. I've spoken to people in particular last year; I spoke to quite a few people who were in the third year of their studies. And normally, it comes to the point where I'm speaking to them right at the end of their third year when they're starting to look. But last year, I spoke to people who were sort of, you know, in the beginnings of their third year and thinking, well, it looks like I'm going to be doing a lot of my lectures on Zoom.

And I might be able to do a job whilst I'm doing the third year of the course. And I have actually placed somebody who's in that position. And they're managing the course, and the job and the employer have been really flexible about giving them the time to finish their course. So that's worked really well, but I think nurturing people is about helping them know what's going to make them stand out from the crowd. They're already standing out because there's not a huge amount of young broadcast technology graduates. So there's a few to choose from for an employer, but there's not that many employers that are going to try and snap them up.

I mean, I was having to think about this, Ben, because we were talking about it before, about how many companies hire graduates and some have their apprenticeship schemes, and some do it kind of ad hoc as they need to. And some do it as a matter of course because budget-wise, it works better for them to get people in fresh, train them up. You know, perhaps don't pay them as much as other companies might, but it works well for them.

It may not work well for them actually retaining that talent once the guys are trained up, they may kind of move on. But I think it's important to talk to the graduates about what makes them stand out. What makes them one of the ones who will get hired if there's not many jobs to choose from? How do you make yourself be the person that gets picked? And, you know, it's got to start with your CV because that's the first thing people see, and you've got to get a foot in the door.

And I know companies; I'm trying to speak without giving too much away because a lot of what I do is confidential. But a company I worked with last year had two CV's for a graduate position, and the CV's were from people from the same university on the same course. And they interviewed one and hired one, and just the difference in the CV is one was more, I guess, more relaxed, chatty almost about "I've done this", "I've done that". And the other one just came across as somebody with a more technical brain because it was, you know, "these are the things I've worked with", "these technologies I've worked with". And "when I did this particular role" whether it was a university or a bit of work experience, "I did this" and "these were the technologies I worked with", And the other one was "I worked with a team of people", I did this, I did that, but it was very, I don't want to say woolly, cause that's not fair, but much more relaxed in style. And the more technical CV got the interview, got the job and the other person didn't get a chance for an interview, which wasn't really fair because they were probably both really good candidates, but I think that's useful.

Another thing that will make people stand out from the crowd, and I don't know how well this will work in COVID times, but off their own back got a load of work experience along with their course, that always works really well. And I can't think of anybody that I've ever dealt with that has got a load of work experience on their CV and hasn't got a job straight away. Cause I think that it just shows how willing you are to put yourself out and do stuff and obviously how much more experience you've gained. I think you know because you're a graduate and you don't have a lot of experience, people at interviews aren't expecting you to have a lot of experience.

So they're not going to throw a load of technical questions at you and expect all the answers. They're going to try and gauge what you know, what you've learned. But what they want to see is, is an aptitude for learning and a proactive attitude. And honesty, really so if you don't know something, you don't try and blag, you know, because you think that's what they want. They just want to know where your knowledge is and what gaps to fill, but I think it's, you know, at that stage, it's all about attitude.

'Broadcast Media: The Inside Track' Podcast published 15th February 2021 on various platforms

Review, Research, Repeat

If your interview went well, then great, but it doesn't stop there. You may find, on average, 20 applications might give you one interview, and it could take five or half a dozen interviews to secure a job. Now think of it as getting in your groove, and you have a cookie-cutter approach to your broadcast search that you can rinse and repeat.

Don't take your foot off the gas; keep going and keep your options open. What you need to do now is nurture the search and keep generating leads. This is where you go back to the industry sources, look at openings and repeat what you've been doing to get you to that stage. This not only applies to your applications for roles but also the search wraparound things, the support aspects, and the meetings and diary items—keep all those up, as it's all part of the same momentum.

Expand your Search

You need to expand your search next, go forth and spread your message. Find a way to your audience in a natural way by word of mouth, summarize and sell your message. Explore their needs, link them to your benefits and leverage your next contact. If you have your target matrix, look at the number of contacts you have in that organization. You can have primary, secondary, tertiary contacts, but look at which ones you might be able to leverage.

Look at the job roles that are being advertised, take note of any industry news or insightful information you can get. This is how you can help tailor your message to them and try to get the inside track of their needs. It's important to go with the gut feelings and any flags that may present themselves. Pursuing these is never bad essentially, and you should always put your trust in your own inner self, and you'll tend to find that most times it's always right.

Cultivate Leads

Cultivating leads by just continuously enforcing your message, remember the 'who am I?' Give out your cards at trade shows and networking events, get LinkedIn connections there and then in person or online. People like the personal style, so if you build up some conversation and rapport and you've got some things in common, connect straight away.

Keep maintaining your matrix, make sure it's updated after you've made some inquiries, and add contacts for the people in your target job role. This may also glean some information on how they got there or what current developments they're working on and having combed through your contact list, then your target companies.

Be active, look for relevant or contacts you need to keep current. Some of these may be passive, so they may not reply too often, but it may be worth looking at some old friendships that may kindle something. These are often people who wouldn't mind hearing from you, academics, old colleagues, growth friends, etc. So these could be people possibly in other industries that you've known for a long time that may help you indirectly to give you fresh perspective or insights.

The Next Opportunity to Talk

Strike while the iron's hot, don't leave a conversation hanging there, why not meet up for lunch, go for a coffee with one of your targets in your network? Say I'll give you a quick ring and just have a phone call with them or an exchange by instant message if that feels easier. Follow up from the interviews, what actions are you going to take? Why not book demonstrations, say hello at networking events, attend their trade show stands? Whilst you're at events and meetings and making connections, send some follow-up emails. Ask if you can visit the premises, say you'd be interested in seeing the products, and inquire about future events.

Get on the social media and networking sites, as a lot of companies are out there, a lot of professional broadcast colleagues; industry contacts are on LinkedIn and other niche platforms. Give them a few likes, shares, give a valuable or light-hearted comment, as that will instigate some communication. Interact with them, try and tease out how they got there, or for example, did they attend the same webinar recently—try to find some common ground.

One thing you should also probably do is to Google yourself; if you are applying, a lot of people are interested in how you turn up in the search results. So if this is turning up some of your student party days or something less professional, then you may want to take down some social media profiles if you want to make it a professional encounter the next time you talk.

Are you more comfortable the more you interact with people, then keeping up the pace of job search is easier - how are you going to keep that drive to secure the role?

Ancast Insight

I'd like to give you a bit of insight into one quiet spell in 2017; my diary had never been so full, actually. There were fortunately quite a lot of trade shows happening over summer, so lots of meetups, DevOps events, cloud trade shows, but I was also arranging demos, lunches with all the industry contacts, as well as the routine search stuff. When I look back at the calendar entries during that period, they were like: Google next show, workshop bank, business development, networking, interview two, go to webinars, social media, courses, digital conference, coffee, lunch, end of year show, and it goes on and on.

So the point I'm trying to make is there's always something to do in your career search. Treating it like that full-time nine-to-five job and by actually having some of those titles in your diary, it gives you some focus time. Some of them I needed to make sure I got done, and so assigned time to do those tasks. Being sure of your competency, of where you want to work, keeping your mantra, and talking as if you're in the job title or role when you are meeting with your next contacts really does show, as it leaves a lasting impression on people.

There are some creative networking events that I've been to called 'Glug' events in London, but in a quiet period, I tried a related industry event. I was trying all sorts of avenues; I explained to people there who I am: "I'm a project engineer." I'd have some of my stories lined up, and I was just practicing essentially, but it reinforced what I was looking for and who I am. It worked, and I got some introductions by speaking to mutual contacts that then understood to refer me: "You should speak to this girl here." It could just be a random LinkedIn connection, but you never know, so keep this up whilst you're in any type of setting.

I think this is now in my subconscious, but self-actualizing my full potential, the "no job" mindset wasn't disheartening, and before long, I then had a number of options, and I chose the best one. It takes just one thought, vision, or dream before you then start realizing your full potential by doing these activities and cultivating these contacts and nurturing these interactions.

9. TRANSITION

Transition to New Role

So you're in luck and start negotiating offers either on the interview day if you've been impressed or a follow-up with the offer coming by phone or mail.

Negotiating with Offers

It's never worth playing multiple prospects off against each other, as they will have backup options anyway. It could also backfire on you in one way or the other at some point down the line. So with the offers, try and understand your own ballpark figure, but the good news is they want you for the role and the ball's in your court now. With all things considered from advice, the additional benefits, and what you know to be reasonable and are comfortable with—just don't keep them hanging too long!

If you're a consultant or freelance contractor or basically self-employed, you must know your worth and what day rate you can command (using industry averages as a guide). This comes with many years of experience, the more of this you have in a particular skill set then, the more in demand you will be. So, in turn, the better day rate you can expect to have, if you're worth it, then the client will pay, but you must be able to back that up with a proven track record.

Clarifications Needed

You may have to work out any clarifications like notice periods if you're transitioning from another role into a new broadcast media role. Start dates for the position you're applying for could be a while off, like a month or two away, or it could be you start on Monday if self-employed. There are plenty of instances where I've interviewed one week, and then the next week, I'm on the assignment and being a consultant up and running by lunchtime!

It's always good to clarify any pre-booked holiday commitments upfront, so this should be mentioned along with any acceptance of the job role just to give some forewarning. Also, clarification around any additional benefits packages such as healthcare packages, or a company pension, any transport perks, or perhaps salary sacrifices for things like seasonal rail passes. Get confirmation of the offer in writing or an email that would give you confidence that you are being offered the role and to confirm your compensation for that.

Keep Your Search Up

So, before you wind down any other searches that you might be on, keep in mind you could still be waiting for written confirmation reliant on other things. There could be some background checks, perhaps, and some employers do this these days if you work with young or vulnerable people. There could be NDAs (non-disclosure agreements) to sign. This is especially the case dealing with talents, celebrities, or some intellectual property involving technology designs.

These are all things you've got to clarify and make sure you dot the I's and cross the T's because until you're working on day one of the jobs, just keep calm and carry on. Nothing is certain unless you've sat in your seat in the new role, so keep your foot firmly on the gas and continue as you have until the ink is dry on the contract.

This would mean keeping your network on warm standby and keeping the matrix maintained and all the other search activities. You could have more interviews lined up, and these should go ahead if nothing has been signed, sealed, and delivered.

The Inside Track

An excerpt from Ancast's podcast with Stephen Furness giving his real-life insight.

Stephen Furness: I'd say go get it, go get it. Don't be shy about it, apply for everything you can, you know, look for the opportunities and make your own luck. It's so important and anyone who's reading should think about what I've just said. What I would say on a more general level is that you must understand the business you're getting into.

That's one of the reasons for doing stuff that was an experience, it's not just the work element, it's just sort of the rationale and everything behind it, you know? So I think there's a lot of people who have a sort of mystical view of what we do and think it's all glamour. But I can assure you stood about in the back of a broadcast compound when it's raining at 10 o'clock at night is not sexy, it's definitely not. So I think there's a lot of value there for people to understand what it is you're wanting to do.

I think the opportunities are different for people now; people won't necessarily have to come to London anymore to achieve certain things. That's a big, big plus for a lot of people who are not based in a capital city and maybe can't manage to move here for whatever reason. I think that's a great leveler, and that's good, that's good news for the business and it will mean a lot of changes.

So a substantial change in how production is made and also we'll open up a lot of opportunities for people that wouldn't have existed previously.

'Broadcast Media: The Inside Track' Podcast published 19th April 2021 on various platforms

Manage Offers and Enquiries

Are you happy to accept? Well, you've got time to reflect before you message or call them back, so think of any conditions or any negotiation before both parties agree.

So you've got some trusted people and their opinion, you're the front-runner and have negotiated well to create a win-win situation; this is what you should be aiming for. Think about the remuneration, aside from salary and daily rate but also the bonuses too. Is there anything that you need to think about, like probation periods, job titles, and description? Would you want to specify anything like that? Confirm there are no further interviews, or would you need to speak to the hiring manager's manager, for example.

If you have multiple offers coming in at the same time, make sure they are managed well. So politely decline the other ones if you have a firm offer in writing and then wind down your search. The key thing at this point is although your search for a new job role is now complete, your career lasts longer than one position.

Maintain Your Network

So, you have landed that ideal role in broadcast media, and all you have to do now for the rest of your working life is just turn up and do the job. Well, things change, so you should think of how to manage all that effort you put into getting the role and make sure it's put to good use.

It could literally be just talking with your colleagues, clients, or suppliers—be enthusiastic, knowledgeable, and personable. You tend to find the cottage industry of broadcasting the people like the soft side; they'll want the small talk and the chit chat so that will build trust and rapport. If you make good impressions on people by being easy to work with and producing some great things for the company, the team, or the client, it'll be remembered. Think of this as low-level networking where you're not actually looking for a new job but have the tone and demeanour that you are; it projects well and shows your professional side.

The next level that takes a lot more effort is to continue the pace you generated during the search for that place in broadcast. This will reinforce your passion for the industry and the role you have in it; you can still update your blog, portfolio, podcast, and LinkedIn while pivoting your message to simple engagement with your network. You need to balance this and ensure you do not appear to be looking for a new job, as quite often, you'll be Googled, LinkedIn and generally new colleagues may take note, so keep it purely maintenance.

What you tend to find is if it's done the right way, then the people who you work with will appreciate mutual industry contacts and previous connections, as it reinforces your drive and outward-looking nature. They will also vouch for you if they know you well enough, which is even better, so rather than just be 'happy in role' and competent in your job, it gives you the edge to have these industry contacts that help in situations that involve career progression.

You may find a happy medium between these 2 examples and have the soft skills and low-level networking by default and then perhaps visit a trade show once a year or go on LinkedIn once a month or accept a networking invite. How far you go in broadcast media all depends on how far you want to take it; it's there for the taking, so tailor your maintenance level that closely fits your ambitions.

So what will your network look like in the future? Remember, things may change, and the only person who is in charge of your career is yourself. So inform recruiters, adjust your online message, tidy up your LinkedIn, take any references off your personal or business websites. Update any online portals, that sort of thing, so you don't get any unnecessary enquiries, especially if your new workplace notices.

Keep Up With The Industry

The other thing linking up with this is keeping up with the industry. It's always useful to keep abreast of the industry news and events. You can still interact with the social platforms, as it's your new job role and survey the workplace for avenues and opportunities. It's also part of the job; you will often be canvassed by your team or client about the latest broadcast trends, technology, and ways of working operationally, so add to the conversation by keeping tabs on the latest.

The key people you can align with will be absorbed into your network, almost by default. Make sure you start off well; the first three months are crucial, most likely the probation period. This works slightly differently if you're a contractor, freelancer, or consultant. So, you want to check for any exit clauses on the client-side and on your side, check the duration of the contract.

The Inside Track

An excerpt from Ancast's podcast with Brad Dickson giving his real life insight.

Brad Dickson: Well, if I'm good at all at my craft, I will say that I owe that to the people who were there before me, right. So that's one thing that it gives is some sort of succession in the sense that, you know, I got the skills from people who started in television, right. And the benefit was that if I was doing something wrong or I was trying something, whatever, at least the solution was there from the senior people. The other benefit now, CBC's model has changed, has gone into more of a freelance model. The one downside with that is that you don't get the succession.

Like I've got 37 years of experience, I've done everything from multi-camera to cinema, to everything, right. And those skill sets that I learned, right - who do I pass them onto? Right, if all of a sudden you're only working with me for a day, like, you know, let's just say our crews should be freelance. If you're only working for a day or a week, it's like, okay, you get to learn that particular show that we're working on.

But if all of a sudden you're not there on another show, you don't get to learn that. So that's what I've found is a bit of a downside going to going to that model. So as I say it is longevity, I did everything from soup to nuts, so to speak.

'Broadcast Media: The Inside Track' Podcast published 12th April 2021 on various platforms

Starting off Well

Easier said than done, whether it's a new freelance starter on a project or a permanent full-time position, be on time, participate, get feedback, listen and learn. Go above and beyond the expectations and build relationships; this is almost like you're giving some preparation for your next revision of your CV. Some of the things you'll start to do in your new job role will be featured on your future CV. So these things where you've performed above expectation, this is crucial. It's worth mentioning that even beyond broadcast media, the probation periods are generally built into the contracts, so you must bring your A-game for the first few months. This is a continuous loop with freelancers, contractors, and consultants in broadcast—as their reputation is on the line and contracts will generally have short exit clauses.

It doesn't stop there when you secure the role as you will develop yourself further, until you retire you must think how will I make sure I'm always happy in my role?

Ancast Insight

There are so many instances to choose from, but from my experience, you've gone and done it after many applications, and countless leads, and many interviews. Travelling across town or to multiple cities and you get an offer from both parties who seem a good fit. This is where you need to ensure you're comfortable with the remuneration, the contract type, the benefits on offer, and the entitlements. Ask the question: does it fit or exceed you or your family's life better? Is that a good move essentially? Because once committed and as soon as you start day one, then you have to prove your worth. You should be eager to do so, and after the initial trial period (if on the payroll), it is the gateway to a long and fruitful employment in broadcast media.

Similar to short self-employed contracts, it could lead to extensions or future work, too, as I've discovered with being hired back for different roles at different times. Looking back on my operations roles, consultancy assignments, or contractor gigs, even though I've moved on, our mutual industry links with people still exist today but with different companies. Like when I was full-time employed with a broadcast service provider called Arqiva, I knew them from years before that from when I worked on an outside broadcast producing the Bollywood Awards. I always remember the name on the truck and the company-branded London underground plastic credit card style map.

I always remember keeping it as a keepsake, and then I remember getting invited for an interview after somebody who was working at Arqiva found me. It was for a shift role and was with them for many, many years, but then having left, got invited back as a consultant on a project internationally. Once that had wound down, I came back to the UK and was offered some more work as a freelance broadcast contractor. This was extended, as they got me involved in training their new shift operators and senior play-out staff as well. So that's one example where I've proven my worth, and I've been invited back multiple times based on the quality of the work, so it's a winning formula, and it can be for you too.

10. EPILOGUE

Epilogue

For me, it's linking new entrants' problems to the career search commitments; I was also in the same place as many of the readers are now. I associate the predicament that you're maybe in right now with the position I was in years ago. It's important not to be lost in the weeds, feeling disheartened and wondering if you're doing the right thing. If you've got a good work ethic and you can apply that to your career search, then you can benefit from the guidance and the insight I try to bring. I want to be the conduit between the new broadcast media entrants and getting them to commit wholeheartedly to their broadcast media career search and all that entails.

Closing Comments

It's fine to be yourself, to know your limits and job expectations, and do what you feel is best and ultimately what makes you happy.

The Inside Track

An excerpt from Ancast's podcast with Jose Otero giving his real-life insight.

Jose Otero: I mean first of all, you have to be true to yourself. Like you have to know - what do you want? You know with this new career that you're getting yourself into, if you know, how far are you willing to take it? And no answer is right, I mean not one answer is right - I think all the answers are correct; it's just the best one that fits your expectations. I've learned about people that are very good broadcasters or very good reporters, but they want to stay where they are because they want to report to the community, and they have a commitment to their community. And that's fine, I mean, that's very honorable as well.

In my case, you know, I wanted to professionally jumpstart my career. And knowing in Puerto Rico at that time, it was impossible for me - I made the decision to move. I've worked with people that right out of college, they decided to look for a bigger market or just, you know, start somewhere else. And that's fine too, but I think that's a decision that is very personal and it's just how do you want to take your career moving forward? You know, again, like I said, some people, they want to stay in their communities. They want to provide a service to their community and that's very honorable as well.

And some people, they just want to focus on their career, in my case I do at some point contemplate returning back to Puerto Rico and give them the knowledge that I learn here and grow, you know, my community and, and how do we inform our community. So it's kinda like, you know for me I chose this path because it's going to give me more resources that I'm going to return. Then, you know, it's, it's going to be better for us.

'Broadcast Media: The Inside Track' Podcast published 22nd February 2021 on various platforms

Ancast Insight

Some thoughts, to sum up, I guess, so there you have it—it's a sort of brain dump of inspiration that I can pass on to graduates and people coming into the broadcast media industry. The practical tips and real-world examples are here to help you and to provide some inspiration on how this may work for you as well. I've worked in education, multimedia, online media, production, and broadcast and have been fortunate to have some of the most rewarding points in my career. So I'm using it to pass on the baton and hope that somebody somewhere found something useful and gained an advantage, however small in their career search and progression.

You may not know when the turns in the road will come, but you can certainly try to make them surface themselves by being driven and persevering. So it's not necessarily about having a foolproof plan, but it's trying things out, experimenting with what works and what doesn't.

Personal Narrative

I've tried to convey the "If you could do it again…" conversation with all my podcast guests, and the book is my attempt at writing it down. Most of the interviewees on the show are taken aback when asked, "If you could talk to your younger self—what would you tell yourself?"

The Inside Track

An excerpt from Ancast's podcast with Laura Whitaker giving her real-life insight.

Ben Anchor: And I'd be interested to know what, if you could tell your 18-year-old self something now, what would it be? What advice would you give your sort of younger self?

Laura Whitaker: The one thing that probably at one point did hold me back as a freelancer in particular. So not in work, but as a freelancer as the internet developed and all these creatives - so Instagram came, Pinterest came and you had access to all of this mountain of work, which was amazing, but also highly intimidating to go up against.

So anyone who's starting out, they will see all of this work and think where on earth do I fit in? So all of that with the skill level that I'm at at the moment, and I'd say, just say that. You really just need to be yourself and realize that you as a person are very unique, you, you will produce something unique. It may be at the start, you may find that you replicate work that you've done before, but over time it will start to become more you and more unique and you will find your own style. And I think that's something that I found quite tricky to find my own style.

'Broadcast Media: The Inside Track' Podcast published 1st February 2021 on various platforms

Having that passion that all of us have in the broadcast media industry, applying that as much to your competency, competency skills, and the search techniques that go with that for your next career move. Just to add a bit of narrative around that by saying I like to 'pay it forwards' in a sense. It's not if, but when you get your dream job, and I found that learning my personal values, behaviours and strengths really helped me as well as developing the broadcast competencies. I'd built these up from being a teenager, going through university, and then getting some soft skills later on to complement those. But it was really when I reflected on myself and learnt a bit more about myself that I was really able to push on and find the type of work that really satisfies me.

Ancast Insight

Time for a bit of a retrospective, I mean, my twenties were great, but even from high school, I never fully knew what I wanted to do long-term after the whirlwind of the undergraduate degree. It was more pronounced after post-graduate, and I felt sort of stuck in a rut, so I thought I was drifting slightly. I was doing something in the same vein that I felt was the right type of work, but I didn't feel content and fully satisfied with what I was doing.

So, I read some books that some people at networking events had suggested about launching business ideas and going self-employed. Some of these books mentioned getting your mojo back, that kindred spirit. I had to basically reinvent myself, so I went to broadcast exhibitions, staying at hostels in London, getting cheap train tickets very, very far in advance, travelling on the bus between the hostel and the exhibition centre. I really wanted this to work, and I wanted to explore all the avenues possible to get me there. So I figured out I had a broad landing space and working in a TV head end is the best visualization I had for this; it could have been something like TV network control or transmission, something like that.

I found a few professional qualifications that were aligned to it, and I self-studied and passed, and before long, I had interviews, and this was during the 2008 financial crash. Thinking back, I was emailing everyone, pushing the communications from all angles. I was staying up even on Friday evenings and sending emails out; I remember one reply from ITV wishing me luck at 9 pm on a Friday thinking, "Wow, a reply late on a Friday night—thanks!" Also, going for some jobs in Manchester that were similar, but not similar enough, perhaps through destiny or luck, an interview in London came up and was just up my street.

And that was it, I had my mojo back! Imagine it's like the first day of uni, everything's new and exciting, but doing this perpetually now in your search. It's as if I had unlimited avenues, doors to knock on, the places I could connect with people. Once you get in it and look back, it will seem like a sort of liberating period of transition.

Although you may seem vulnerable and you may have a burden of responsibility, sometimes even desperation, it's a very, very dynamic time, and you are controlling your own destiny at that point. The one thing to remember about that is finding that spark inside you, knowing the world is yours. That seems to last through your university years, and you need to find it and keep the pilot light on as you move through your career.

Inspirational Speech

Steve Jobs

"Your work is going to fill a large part of your life, and the only way to be truly satisfied is to do what you believe is great work. And the only way to do great work is to love what you do. If you haven't found it yet, keep looking. Don't settle. As with all matters of the heart, you'll know when you find it."

"You can't connect the dots looking forward; you can only connect them looking backwards. So you have to trust that the dots will somehow connect in your future. You have to trust in something—your gut, destiny, life, karma, whatever. This approach has never let me down, and it has made all the difference in my life."

JK Rowling

"You've got to work. It's about structure. It's about discipline. It's all these deadly things that your schoolteacher told you needed… You need it."

"I believe in hard work and luck, and that the first often leads to the second."

Ancast Insight

The only person who's in charge of your career is you, not the university, not your boss, not your parents. Always trust your gut, the flags in your mind, and use these to take you on your path. Hard decisions you can sleep and reflect on, keep searching for the work that really makes you happy; you'll know when you find it.

Some of the unexpected events lead to the most fruitful sometimes. Many times, it will be a call out of the blue that you're waiting to receive, and it surprises you. In the meantime, keep on keeping on, go forth and be who you want to be.

Author's Bio

 Ben Anchor is a creative & media technology graduate and accomplished broadcast consultant who wrote the book "The Broadcast Media Inside Track."

The book is all about the industry-wide aspects not taught in any curriculum and instead uses real life experience from both him and guest contributors. Coining the phrase it's 'paying it forwards' to the new generation in broadcast media and get that edge in their career search.

He's a Master of Science postgraduate in Creative Technology at Leeds Beckett University before forging a career in broadcast media. His journey includes experience with production, post-production, TV transmission, lecturing, broadcasters, service providers, cloud computing and projects in the capacity of freelance, full time employee and and his own consultancy. You can find more info and his podcast at **ancast.co.uk/podcast**

Based out of the bustling and compact London, he always finds time for a cycling trip outside of the city in the mountains as well as touring around the UK or Europe. A bit further afield, he's always soaking up culture worldwide, especially by travelling through the 7 continents on his winter trips.

Afterword

The book had been in the making for a while; during some downtime in 2017, I started to plan out the structure and at least the table of contents. Some broadcast work then picked up at that point, and although the momentum was lost, the idea remained, waiting in the wings. It took until the COVID-19 pandemic of early 2020 for the manuscript to be dusted off and the writing process done, and editing finished in 2021.

It coincided with a few other publishing works at the time; I was writing articles, posting social content, authoring training materials, and producing my own podcast series. Through all this copywriting, dealing with content, and talking with people from all over the industry, it seemed like the stars aligned and the book should be finished.

I was looking at the calendar, contemplating the length of the pandemic and what could I do to keep my resiliency and help those in the industry in a less fortunate position. So, launching the podcast episodes from February to May 2021, this would help newcomers weekly, then by summer, the book would be ready, as many graduates would be leaving their courses.

And with self-publishing, an accessible option, and electronic and print on demand, distributors providing friendly services means that I can pay it forwards to you all.

Acknowledgements

To start with the people who were involved from the start and who helped inspire me and keep on making me feel that it's worthwhile:

- Thomas J Southerton – longtime friend, hosted me on every trip to Japan and an inspiration to achieve so much in challenging times. We were all systems go in the 2020 pandemic and he tended to constant updates to the book as well as taking the Ancast portfolio up a level.

- Natsu Fukano – always impressed with any graphic work and could turn things round with my guidance. As the creative briefs increased, so did the quality - really happy with the illustrations of me in glasses!

There are some other confidants that I called on from time to time in the authoring world, and glad they got my back:

- Tanya Focus – what I call a 'growth' friend who inspires by default and provides help and support mentally and practically. She's my wing woman and was publishing her own book and so gave me great advice.
- Paul Parry – always available for a quick chat and always followed up with attachments and links. We worked together in the broadcast industry too, so gave invaluable feedback to get me ready to publish.

List of Contributors

The unexpected input was from the guests I hosted on my podcast show; having read the transcriptions, I felt some excerpts had to go in. So in no particular order, here are the selected guests who were happy to pay it forwards too:

- Grace Amodeo – a new LA connection, Grace summed up perfectly that every role on set is important, not just directors.
- Melissa Carr – longtime associate and well placed to give us tips on getting into broadcast professional services.
- Phil Hodgetts – I liked Phil talking about your internal compass or 'north star' as he calls it, something that's untaught.
- Michael Kosmides – a new academic acquaintance, Michael explains getting in the right mindset, thinking 'you are a broadcast journalist.'
- Natasha Monaghan – my first recruiter, what I liked is Natasha talking about where newcomers' strengths are in the interview.
- Stephen Furness – my latest connection, Steve has been around the block, so he tells us how it is – it's not all glamourous!
- Brad Dickson – a new Canadian connection, although retired, Brad recounts the importance of longevity in your career roles.
- Jose Otero – always full of life, Jose has the skills that mix people and technology, and I can see he wants to pay it forwards too.

- Laura Whitaker – an academic connect, we go way back; I like how she explains finding your own style starting out young.

www.ingramcontent.com/pod-product-compliance
Lightning Source LLC
LaVergne TN
LVHW011712060526
838200LV00051B/2885